Michael Baur

T0145394

Steps to Reconciliation
Reformed and Anabaptist Churches in Dialogue

T V Z

Michael Baumann (Ed.)

Steps to Reconciliation
Reformed and Anabaptist
Churches in Dialogue

T V Z

Theologischer Verlag Zürich

Further documentation, graphics and news can be found at
www.anabaptist.ch.

Translation from German:
Lanette Meister, Mike Gray and others

The German version is available under:
Michael Baumann (Hg.):
Gemeinsames Erbe. Reformierte und Täufer im Dialog
ISBN 978-3-290-17430-9
© 2007 Theologischer Verlag Zürich

Die Deutsche Bibliothek – Bibliografische Einheitsaufnahme
Die Deutsche Bibliothek verzeichnet diese Publikation in der Deutschen
Nationalbibliografie; detaillierte bibliografische Daten sind im Internet
über http://dnb.ddb.de abrufbar.

Umschlaggestaltung:
Simone Ackermann, Zeljko Gataric, Zürich
Druck:
Rosch-Buch, Scheßlitz

ISBN 978-3-290-17451-4
© 2007 Theologischer Verlag Zürich
www.tvz-verlag.ch

Statement of Regret

The Reformed churches and the Anabaptist movement are all essentially branches on one and the same bough of the great Christian tree. Both are offspring of the Reformation. Right from the start however they went their separate ways, so that a tragic rift ran through the Zurich Reformation, painful traces of which are discernable to this day. Executions, persecution and expulsions were carried out to eliminate the Anabaptist movement. Yet it has survived and is still flourishing today. The descendants of those early Anabaptists are a living testimony to this.

The persecuted do not forget their history; the persecutors by contrast would prefer to do so. We – representatives of the Reformed State Church of the Canton of Zurich – acknowledge that our church has largely suppressed the story of the persecution of the Anabaptists.

We confess that the persecution was, according to our present conviction, a betrayal of the Gospel and that our Reformed forefathers were in error on this issue.

We affirm that the judgment against the Anabaptists in the *Second Helvetic Confession*, which discards the teaching of the Anabaptists as unbiblical and refuses any communion with them, is no longer valid for us and that it is now our earnest desire to discover and strengthen our common ties.

We acknowledge the faithful of the Anabaptist tradition as our sisters and brothers and their churches as part of the body of Christ, whose diverse members are united through the Spirit of God.

We honor the radical approach of the Anabaptist movement to be the salt of the earth and the light of the world as a free community of committed believers putting into practice the message of the Sermon on the Mount.

It is time to accept the history of the Anabaptist movement as part of our own, to learn from the Anabaptist tradition and to strengthen our mutual testimony through dialogue.

Following the example of our Reformed tradition, *we confess*:

We do not belong to ourselves. We belong to Jesus Christ who calls us to follow him and to be reconciled with those brothers and sisters who have any just reasons to reproach us.

We do not belong to ourselves. We belong to Jesus Christ who reconciles us with God through his death on the cross and has committed to us the ministry of reconciliation.

We do not belong to ourselves. We belong to Jesus Christ who tore down the wall of enmity and united people near and far in one body.

Table of Content

Foreword

Both Reformed and Mennonite churches trace their beginnings back to Zurich, where Huldrych Zwingli and his closest co-workers and friends Konrad Grebel and Felix Manz together discovered a force in the liberating Gospel that would renew both church and society. However, they quickly developed conflicting ideas about how to carry out this renewal. Their paths separated into dispute. Zurich became the «city of Zwingli» and banished the names of Felix Manz and Konrad Grebel from its memory. Still, the Anabaptist movement survived and never forgot its founding fathers. On June 26, 2004, Felix Manz returned to Zurich: a commemorative plaque on the banks of the Limmat reminds us of his execution during the time of the Reformation. This is a reference to an inheritance which Reformed and Anabaptist Christians have in common – and is likewise an encouragement to brotherly dialogue. Both churches have developed the Reformation inheritance differently. However today, in an ecumenical spirit and with mutual esteem, they are learning from each other, sharing their gifts and together trying to give testimony to the Gospel in church and in society.

We thank everyone who prepared and ran the conference day of June 26, 2004, namely Philippe Dätwyler, Peter Dettwiler, Thomas Gyger, Hanspeter Jecker, Elisabeth Lutz-Hellstern and John E. Sharp as well as Michael Baumann for his work on this document.

Thankful for every step of reconciliation and bound by faith in Jesus Christ

Ruedi Reich
President of the Council
of the Evangelical-Reformed Church
of the Canton of Zurich

Paul Gerber
President of the Swiss
Mennonite Conference

Introduction

Michael Baumann

In the summer of 2004 as part of the festivities surrounding Heinrich Bullinger's 500th birthday, representatives of the Reformed church met with Anabaptists from Switzerland, Europe and overseas. It was not the first meeting between Anabaptist churches and the Reformed; however, it was certainly the most profound to date and was in many respects a landmark.

The statement of regret printed at the beginning of this short publication expresses the central goals of the Reformed representatives. They aimed at acknowledging the Anabaptist churches as sister churches, at discovering commonalities in both of these Reformation traditions and at paying homage to those who suffered under the violence of the church of the 16th century, perpetrated in the name of a false understanding of the Gospel.

The reading of this confession in the Zurich Grossmünster by *Ruedi Reich*, President of the Council of the Reformed Church of Zurich, was the central moment in the encounter – and the first part of this work, containing historical and theological articles about the history of the Anabaptist movement and the Reformed church, connects to it. In a longer contribution *Peter Dettwiler* summarizes the disastrous history of the Anabaptist persecution, followed by initially hesitant, then more decisive steps toward a reconciliation between the sibling churches. *Hanspeter Jecker* examines the central differences between the two ecclesiological models from a Mennonite perspective. In two subsequent articles *Peter Dettwiler* presents ways of bringing the dialogue between Anabaptists and Reformed to greater fruition. The chapter «New Horizons» presents several personal reactions from American Mennonites demonstrating the significance of the conference in Zurich. The first part ends with a short perspective in which *Michael Baumann* sketches out some consequences of the historical research and theological dialogue for the Reformed position, particularly as regards the question of baptism.

Part two presents the documents of the conference itself. It begins from a Mennonite perspective with *Larry Miller's* sermon in the Grossmünster, followed by the Reformed statement of regret accompanied by a response from Swiss Mennonites. *Pierre Bühler's* eleven theses about differences and common ground in the way Anabaptist communities and the Reformed state church understand ecclesiology – that is, the church – effectively summarize the dialogue. Afterwards *Philippe Dätwyler* provides transcripts of the speeches made at the dedication of the commemorative stone for the Anabaptists who were once drowned in the Limmat. It concludes with a moving letter drawn up by the *Old Order Amish Churches* in response to their invitation to the conference in 2004. That this letter comes at the end of the work should by no means be taken to mean that it is less important than the preceding contributions; in fact, the spirit of reconciliation one feels in this document could well be said to bring the document to its climax. The letter demonstrates like no other document that the quarrels and disputes which led to literal bloodshed five hundred years ago can be transformed into an attitude of reconciliation, reciprocal respect, perhaps even loving encounter.

This little book picks up the thread which the conference in Zurich began to spin in the hope that the dialogue between Reformed and Anabaptist Christians can be continued and deepened – and that this may serve as a step toward the reign of peace for which the Reformed and Anabaptists alike have hoped, trusted and toiled since the 16th century.

Zurich, spring 2007

First Part

Reformed and Anabaptist Churches in Dialogue

Mennonites and Reformed – A Process of Reconciliation

Peter Dettwiler

Reformed churches were not only victims of persecution but also became guilty of oppressing and persecuting other Christians. The most systematic and cruel persecution concerned the Anabaptists and Mennonites. In recent times efforts have been made to come to terms with this dark history. The following pages offer a survey of the main steps in the process of reconciliation in which Reformed and Mennonite churches have engaged – at the international level and more particularly in the city of Zurich where the Anabaptist movement played a significant role and where the persecution started in the 16th century.

The Shadows of the Past

The leaders of the Anabaptist movement called for a radical reform. They were not satisfied with reviving the preaching of God's word and reforming the order of worship and religious instruction. They sought to gather communities of genuine Christians. The sign of true rebirth was believer's baptism. From 1525 they assembled in small groups and practiced re-baptism. In their view the Christian community was entirely distinct from society. They refused to serve on the magistrate and were not prepared to take any public oath. They attacked the Reformers and denounced their half-heartedness occasionally in harsh words.

All Reformers rejected the movement. Huldrych Zwingli in Zurich used particularly violent language to describe and judge their «aberration». In his *Explanation of the Christians Faith* (1531) he calls the «sect» a particularly «rotten species of human beings» and even uses terms such as the «plague» or «weed» of the Anabaptists. He was determined to eradicate the movement. In a letter addressed to Joachim Vadian, the Reformer of St. Gallen, two days before the execution of Felix Manz, he writes: «Time has come to throw the Anabaptists to the vultures. They disturb the peace of pious people in this city. But I am confident that the ax is now laid at the root of the tree. God help his Church. Amen.»[1]

Felix Manz, together with Konrad Grebel one of the leaders of the movement in Zurich, was executed on January 5, 1527. He was drowned in the river. In his last letter to the community he wrote: «Love and nothing but love pleases God. Who has no love, has no place with God … Jesus had no feelings of hate towards anybody, and therefore his true servants can never hate anybody but follow Christ on the way on which he has preceded them.»[2]

But persecution and other harsh measures did not succeed in suppressing the movement. The chronicler Sebastian Franck reports in 1531: «They spread so quickly that their doctrine was soon heard everywhere and that they found many followers. They baptized many thousand sincere people longing for God. Through their good reputation and their commitment to the letter of Scripture, which they firmly observe, they attract many. Because they do not

---

[1] Quoted from *Ökumenische Kirchengeschichte der Schweiz*, Freiburg/Basel, 1994, p. 115.

[2] Ibid.

teach only in appearance love, faith and the cross.»[3] In the eyes of the Reformers and of the magistrate the Anabaptists represented a serious threat to the established order. On April 23, 1529 a law was adopted at the level of the Empire threatening all Anabaptists who were not ready to abjure their faith with execution through «fire, glove or similar means» without any further trial. From 1525 to 1751 more than 220 official statements against the danger of the Anabaptists were issued, 59 alone during the first five years of the movement.[4]

The Reformed churches rejected the Anabaptist movement not only in their preaching and teaching but included their condemnation in their confessions of faith. The *Second Helvetic Confession* (1566) summarizes the Reformed position without any hesitation: «We reject all other doctrines of the Anabaptists which represent their own invention and deviate from God's word. We are not Anabaptists and do not have anything in common with them.» The consequence of such official condemnations was that the judgment on the Anabaptists was passed on to subsequent generations and thus became part of «Reformed identity». In the article concerning the magistrate (ch. 30), the *Second Helvetic Confession* even justifies the use of violence against Anabaptists: «The magistrate has the duty to keep within bounds obstinate heretics – as long as they are real heretics – if they do not cease to blaspheme God's majesty and to disturb and even ruin the church.» There can be no doubt that for Bullinger, the author of the *Second Helvetic Confession*, the Ana-

---

[3] Quoted from *Die Täuferbewegung: Eine kurze Einführung in ihre Geschichte und Lehre,* J. C. Wenger, Oncken Verlag, Wuppertal und Kassel 1984, Third edition 1995, p. 109.

[4] Ibid., p. 112.

baptists were to be considered as «obstinate heretics». Already in 1535, appealing to the Bible and Augustin, he had justified in a memorandum the use of violence in dealing with the Anabaptists.

Conflicting Memories

The persecuted do not forget. The perpetrators tend to suppress the dark events of their history. This observation also applies to the relationship between Reformed and Mennonites. Who looks today for historical traces of the two movements in the city of Zurich, will soon become aware of the discrepancy. The South gate of the main church (Grossmünster) in Zurich provides a perfect illustration. A bronze relief recalls in 24 small panels the history of the Reformation. The powerful figure of Zwingli dominates. Two panels are devoted to the first witnesses who were sentenced to death in the 1520s – Hans Wirth, who was beheaded in the city of Baden in 1524, and Pastor Jakob Kaiser, who died on the stake in Schwyz in 1529. To emphasize the continuity with the earliest period of the city of Zurich, Felix and Regula, and their servant Exuperantius, three martyrs of the Roman time, are also given a place on the portal. But the visitor will not find any trace of the Anabaptists.

Monuments have been erected for Huldrych Zwingli and also for his successor Heinrich Bullinger. But until recently the name of Felix Manz, the first Anabaptist to die for his faith could not be found in the city. Zurich opened its doors to many refugees seeking security within its walls. One of the panels of the portal shows the arrival of the refugees from Locarno in the South of Switzerland in 1555 and a tablet on the outside of the church recalls the story and the stay in

Zurich of 30 Hungarian pastors who had been freed from the galleys (1667–1677). An inscription at the entrance to another church in Zurich, the Fraumünster, commemorates the reception of the French Huguenot refugees in 1685. But reference to the fact that the Reformed Church of Zurich has sent into exile hundreds of Anabaptists can only be found in history books. Things began to change after the Second World War. In 1952, at the request of the Fifth Mennonite World Conference the following inscription was placed on the wall of the family home of Konrad Grebel: «In this house lived from 1508 to 1514 and 1520–1525 Konrad Grebel who, together with Felix Manz, founded the Anabaptist movement.» The city government still rejected, however, the proposal to commemorate Manz by some kind of monument. It took more than another fifty years to change this decision. On June 26, 2004, in the year of the 500th anniversary of Bullinger's birth, a commemorative stone was inaugurated on the precise spot where Felix Manz was drowned:

«From a fishing platform here in the middle of the Limmat Felix Manz and five other Anabaptists were drowned between 1527 and 1532, during the time of the Reformation. The last Anabaptist to be executed in Zurich was Hans Landis in 1614.»

Photo One: «Tribute to Hans Landis». James Landis from Petersburg, West Virginia, at the inauguration of the memorial plaque.

At the inauguration a choir of Mennonite and Amish believers from America and Europe sang. James Landis, a direct descendant of Hans Landis in the 14th generation, recited a poem he had written for the occasion.

Stages in the Process of Reconciliation

Persecution through imprisonment, confiscation, expulsion and discrimination continued until the end of the 18th century. The Reformed churches in Switzerland, in particular in Zurich and Berne, copied in many respects the Roman inquisition. They have to admit today that they «could, in their own ways, fall victim to many of the same faults they criticized in the Roman Catholic Church. They provided legitimacy to sometimes oppressive political establishments, fell into clericalism, and grew intolerant of minority viewpoints. They were occasionally guilty of condemnations, burnings and banishment, for example in regard to the Anabaptists in Switzerland, acts in many cases typical of their times but not to be excused on that account.»[5]

In the churches the change came from two sides – from Pietism and the Enlightenment. Though on different grounds, their representatives defended the principle of tolerance. At the level of the state the Helvetic Constitution of 1798 and the «Law of Religious Tolerance» of February 12, 1799 made room for Anabaptist communities. When, in 1815, the former Diocese of Basel became part of the Canton of Berne, the agreement made explicit reference to the Anabaptists: «Their worship will be tolerated on the condition that a) they are prepared … to enter their marriages and births in the public register; b) their promise by handshake has the same juridical force as the solemn oath; c) they are obliged to serve in the army like all other citizens but that they can provide for substitution (§13).»

In 1847 the first Mennonite chapel was inaugurated in Basel, the first of its kind in the whole of Switzerland. From around 1900 historical studies have decisively contributed to a less partisan picture of the Anabaptist movement.[6] The First Mennonite World Conference held in

---

[5] «Towards a Common Understanding of the Church: Reformed – Roman Catholic Dialogue, Second Phase.» 1990, §23, in: Jeffrey, FSC, Harding Meyer, William G. Rusch, *Growth in Agreement II*, Geneva 2000.

[6] In particular Ernst Troeltsch and Ernst Müller, 1895. An important historical study was published by Fritz Blanke, *Brüder in Christo: Die Geschichte der ältesten Täufergemeinde,* 1955, new edition Winterthur 2003. – *Brothers in Christ: The History of the Oldest Ana-*

Basel in 1925 provided the opportunity for encounters with Reformed churches and theological faculties. Reformed theologians referred with regret to the persecutions of the past.

Further steps followed in the Canton of Berne. In 1941 the Mennonite communities were exempted from church taxes and a few years later recognized also by the state as religious communities whose teaching and activities follow the same line as the official church.

All these steps were acts of tolerance which did not yet address the deeper issues raised by the persecutions of the past. The spiritual dimension came to the fore with the rise of the ecumenical movement. Under the impression of the Second World War first official encounters between the Swiss Reformed churches and the Historic Peace churches (Mennonites, Quakers, Church of the Brethren) were organized in the 1940s and 1950s in Pidoux on Lake Geneva. For the first time the Mennonites were taken seriously as ecumenical partners. In the «Swiss Association for the History of the Anabaptists», founded in 1973, Reformed and Mennonite historians collaborated from the very beginning.

An important step was taken in 1983. On March 5, a Day of Encounter took place in the Baptist Theological Seminary of Rüschlikon (near Zurich) under the auspices of the World Alliance of Reformed Churches. To celebrate the successful conclusion of a ten year dialogue with the Baptist World Alliance, delegates not only from Reformed and Baptist but also from Mennonite churches were invited. Papers were read and much time was reserved for

---

baptist Congregation, Wipf and Stock Publishers, Eugene, Oregon, 2003.

personal encounter. The main event of the day was a worship service of reconciliation at the Grossmünster, the main church of Zurich. On this occasion, the President of the Church of Zurich, Pastor Ernst Meili, offered a confession of sin in the form of a prayer:

«Father in Heaven, in you alone we find truth and life. Therefore we come before you today and pray: renew our faith, the assurance of our calling in Jesus Christ and the fellowship with Him and with one another. We thank you for all that your Spirit, since the first days and through the centuries, has brought to pass in your church. We thank you for all those who have witnessed to the gospel through their words and with their lives. We thank you particularly for the Reformers, to whose witness and work the Church owes so much. Yet we confess before you how often we have become deaf to the voice of your Spirit, preferring our own insights and ideas. Today we confess before you and our Mennonite and Baptist sisters and brothers how often we as Reformed Christians have failed to understand the message you desire to be mediated to your Church, by the testimony and work of our fellow Christians in the free church tradition. We bring before you all the injustice done to them in our country throughout the ages: persecution, oppression, execution and banishment. Lord our God, show your grace and your mercy upon us. Forgive and help us today to begin anew in fellowship with one another through the power of reconciliation and love, in order that wounds be healed and fellowship may grow and deepen. Lord have mercy on us.»[7]

The service included the common celebration of the Lord's supper.

The encounter in Zurich led to an international dialogue between the World Alliance of Reformed Churches and the Mennonite World Conference. The purpose of this dialogue was «to listen to one another and talk together about a) our common roots and history, b) our unresolved differences and c) our mission as Churches of Christ in today's world.»[8] The formulation of this triple mandate is helpful for every dialogue between the Reformed and the Mennonites. Encounter can proceed from common roots but must also face the differences in perceiving the history and contribute to the «reconciliation of memories». The theological and especially the ecclesiological differences must not be suppressed but need to be openly discussed; because each Church has its own charisma, which it has to maintain faithfully and to witness to in the ecumenical movement. Dialogue has reached its goal if it succeeds in strengthening the churches in their common mission in and for the world.

In 1983 the *Schweizerische Evangelische Synode*, a representative but temporary and unofficial body of the Swiss Reformed churches, again addressed the issue. A message, issued by the Synod on May 15, explicitly affirms the desire of reconciliation: «We are particularly happy to welcome a Mennonite representative among us. We are aware of the

---

[7]   «Baptists and Reformed in Dialogue», *Studies from the World Alliance of Reformed Churches* no. 4, Geneva 1983, p. 47.

[8]   «Mennonites and Reformed in Dialogue», *Studies from the World Alliance of Reformed Churches* no. 7, Geneva 1986, p. 1.

unspeakable injustice inflicted on them since the time of the Reformation in our country. We are grateful for the sign of forgiveness conveyed by their presence among us.» This very modest statement caused considerable debate. Who is entitled to ask for forgiveness? To what extent can we act on behalf of our ancestors?

In 1988 an exhibition was organized in Berne to commemorate the disputation of 1538 through which relationships were dramatically aggravated. A joint service was celebrated on this occasion. A few years later a very special anniversary took place. When Anabaptists were sent into exile, their property was confiscated and used for financing church buildings, schools and poor-relief. To make possible the construction of the church in 1693, the Bernese government attributed Anabaptist goods to the parish of Schwarzenegg in the Canton of Berne. To mark the anniversary, Mennonite delegates were invited. They were prepared to make peace and did not put forward any reparation claims.

In May 2003 the organization «Schleife» in Winterthur hosted a conference under the title: «Heal Our Land – Steps towards Reconciliation with the Anabaptists.» It was mainly a meeting of charismatic groups from Switzerland and the USA, aiming at the spiritual renewal of their respective churches. The Swiss Mennonite Conference was also invited, and representatives of the Reformed state church also took part in the service of reconciliation in the Zurich Grossmünster. The title of the conference suggests that these «Steps towards Reconciliation» serve a missionary objective: They should clear out a path for God's blessing, so that contemporary churches can experience renewal and testify more powerfully.

In 2004 Schleitheim in the Canton of Schaffhausen was the scene of a further act of reconciliation. In the early 16th century the village was a center of the Anabaptist movement. The Schleitheim articles, the first Anabaptist confession of faith, were published in 1527. The Anabaptists gathered secretly in the mountainous woods. The path leading there is still called the «Täuferstig», the «Anabaptist climb». On March 28 a stone of witness was inaugurated at the end of the path – in the presence of Reformed, Mennonites and free church representatives.

A little later, on June 26, 2004, the Church of Zurich organized as part of the celebrations in memory of Heinrich Bullinger, an international conference under the title «The Reformation and the Anabaptists – Steps to reconciliation». Many Mennonites participated in a program of theological reflection and personal exchange. A service of reconciliation was celebrated. The main element of the event was, no doubt, as already mentioned, the inauguration of a tablet commemorating the execution of Felix Manz and other Anabaptists. The representative of the political authorities called the persecution and execution of Anabaptists an injustice – though he admitted that the reaction of the authorities at that time was understandable as the solidity of the public order seemed to be at stake. The President of the Church of Zurich left no doubt about the stance of the church: «The Reformation in Zurich regarded itself as a rediscovery of the liberating Gospel of Jesus Christ ... We are therefore all the more ashamed and pained that the Reformed church should have become a persecutor ... We acknowledge this historic sin and, from today's point of view, consider it a betrayal of the Gospel. Before God and before men, we point to this dark side of the Reformation, and we ask God and you, dear brothers and sisters of Mennonite faith, to forgive us.»[9] In a statement of faith the Church also addressed the delicate issue of the anathemas in the confessions of faith of the Reformation time: «We affirm that the judgment against the Anabaptists in the *Second Helvetic Confession,* which discards the teaching of the Anabaptists as unbiblical and refuses any communion with them, is no longer valid for us and that it is now our earnest desire to discover and strengthen our common ties.»[10] In response, the representative of the Swiss Mennonite Conference declared: «By inaugurating this rock in the exact same place where Felix Manz and his friends received the blood baptism, and by reaffirming in a lasting form that your predecessors were wrong in the way they treated these dissidents, you are acting in order to reestablish justice ... At one time divided, we want today, in the midst of our society, to join our voices to yours, dear Reformed friends, in order to repeat together the message of Him who touches and transforms hearts, who is no other than Jesus Christ, our Lord!»[11]

Issues to be Considered

The Reformed churches reject without reserve as an aberration the violence perpetrated against the Anabaptists in the course of the centuries. They are prepared to admit the guilt of their Church in this respect. The interpretation of the controversy raises many questions. The view of Reformed and Mennonite historians continue to differ. The

---

[9]   Cf. full text on pp. 93–94.
[10] Cf. full text on pp. 81–82.
[11] Cf. full text on pp. 94–95.

tablet in memory of Felix Manz does deliberately not use the tern «martyr» but simply refers to the fact of the execution. An interpretative presentation of the incident must be the object of a joint effort. To come to terms with the past, Reformed and Mennonite need to reach an understanding of the Reformation which does justice to both sides. Despite the shadows of the past, the Reformed owe to the Reformers essential insights, and the same is true for the relationship of the Mennonites to their spiritual fathers and mothers. Only on the basis of a joint effort can the conflicting memories be «reconciled». The effort begins with each church seeking to view history with the eyes of the other church.

In the perspective of the 16th century the response of the Reformers was understandable. They saw in the Anabaptist movement a threat to their own cause. The internal tensions weakened their movement. «Two parties militate against us, they are as different as they possibly can be. Because what does the party of the Pope have in common with the Anabaptists?» Calvin writes in his answer to the attacks of Cardinal Sadolet in 1539. It is a fact that the acceptance of the Reformation in the city of Solothurn failed because of the tensions between Reformed and Anabaptists. Above all, the movement constituted a threat to the order of society, which was based on the concept that church and state formed a unity. In the city of Zurich of that time no Jews were admitted and when the Reformation was introduced, those who wished to stay with the «old faith» had to emigrate. Religious tolerance is not a child of the Reformation but of the Enlightenment. Fritz Blanke thinks therefore that the vision of a church built on voluntary membership was an experiment which occurred too early, «before the time was ripe. In reality, that was no fault but an heroic deed. There will always be a need for men who, unconfused by the spirit of their age, set out for new goals and strive toward a new dawn ... Their daring hast not been in vain. In gratitude we bow before them today.»[12]

But what then can efforts at reconciliation bring? Critical questions have been raised from both sides. Reformed Christians tend to have a loose relationship with their own history and their confessions of faith, and therefore also have some difficulty in identifying with events of reconciliation. It is interesting to note that the reconciliation service in 1983 was quickly forgotten and new efforts had to be undertaken. The controversies with the Anabaptists simply belong to the past. Reformed Christians tend to give their attention primarily to the pressing challenges in today's world. The lack of a strong sense of tradition leads them to question the duty to accept responsibility for failures of previous generations.

The Mennonite attitude is different because the persecutions of the past have become part of their identity as Anabaptists; they can therefore not be suppressed and forgotten. But in the conversations with the Reformed the Mennonites emphasized that the time of the persecutions has passed and been replaced by a new spirit of mutual ecumenical understanding. They do not wish to be identified with the role of victims. Many controversies which until recently seemed insurmountable have lost their relevance. Believer's baptism is now accepted also in Reformed churches and has been defended by such a prestigious theologian as Karl Barth. Mennonite and Baptist welcome Christians of other churches who have been baptized at the Lord's Supper. Also the controversy over wearing arms has changed its character.

---

[12] See note 6.

In his response to the statement of faith of the Church of Zurich the President of the Swiss Mennonite Conference said on June 26, 2004: «History may designate us as victims, and could incite us to find satisfaction in that. However, those here among you today, descendants of those Anabaptists persecuted in the past, no longer feel as victims. We do not ask for material retribution for the past: that would seem to us to be contrary to the Spirit of the Gospel. But the fact that you recognize the difficult points of your history in relation to ours helps us to see ourselves and to meet you differently. We thank you therefore for your statement and wish to accept it in a spirit of forgiveness ... The plaque that will be unveiled today in this city of Zurich attests that actions have been taken with determination.»[13]

This response points to an important concern of such reconciliation events. The Reformed statement of regret is not only an offer to deeper dialogue and increased collaboration but helps *both* churches to deal with their own past in a self-critical way and thus to relate to the other in greater openness and respect. It gives them the freedom to learn from the strong sides of the other without giving up their own identity. And finally, the dialogue based on steps of reconciliation gives new access to what we have in common. The statement of the Church of Zurich declares: «The Reformed churches and the Anabaptist movement are all essentially branches on one and the same bough of the great Christian tree. Both are offspring of the Reformation.» The same affirmation had already been made in 1986 by the Reformed-Mennonite dialogue: The two churches have common roots and are, in a certain sense, twin sisters.

---

13   Cf. full text on pp. 83–84.

Is this affirmation realistic? The distance between the two churches has not yet been entirely overcome and it is important to recognize that the process of reconciliation has not yet reached its ultimate goal. The proposal to celebrate, as a sign of communion, the Lord's Supper together on June 26 met with some reserve among certain Mennonite and Amish congregations in the USA. They felt that the time had not yet come to share this sign of intimate communion with the Reformed. Such signals must be fully respected.[14]

---

[14] The Old Order Amish Churches of the USA, the most conservative among the Amish groups, did not attend the Conference in Zurich. They sent a friendly message re-affirming their identity as Anabaptists and also questioning the usefulness of «world travel», a challenge which certainly needs to be taken seriously. Cf. full text on pp. 96–97.

Reconciliation? A Mennonite Statement

Hanspeter Jecker

«We do not have anything in common with them!» said Zwingli's successor, Heinrich Bullinger, about the Anabaptists. Does this remain so today? What has happened to the Anabaptists and where do they stand today?

The Mennonite congregations of Switzerland stem from the Anabaptist movement which originated during the time of the Reformation in the early 16th century. They are considered the oldest Protestant free church. In contrast to the authoritarian force model achieved by the state church, the proponents of believer's baptism sought a non-authoritarian congregation based on voluntary membership. Because of this, in Zurich in January of 1525, some former colleagues and friends of Zwingli's began baptizing adults who in this way freely gave testimony to their faith. At about the same time, similar movements, which were as a whole named the «radical Reformation», emerged in other places in Europe.

Through their criticism of what in their eyes was a disastrous alliance of church and state, the Anabaptists soon incurred the wrath of the authorities. Despite the rapid start of persecution, the «Re-baptizers», increasingly called «Mennonites» after their Dutch leader, Menno Simons (1496–1561), rapidly spread first across Europe and then later also to North and South America. However, the confiscation of goods, exile, prison, torture and execution drove the Anabaptists ever deeper into isolation. An increasingly societal, and from time to time also theological, narrowness partly resulted in painful developments. Internal conflicts led to the formation of the stricter and withdrawn Amish movement in 1693.

Photo Two: Anabaptist cave near Bäretswil in the Zurich Oberland, a place of refuge for persecuted Anabaptist communities in the 16th century.

After a new blossoming in the late 16th and early 17th centuries in Zurich, this wing of the «radical Reformation» almost totally disappeared from the scene by 1700 due to intense persecution. One finds traces of Zurich-rooted Anabaptist belief first in Moravia, then in Alsace, in the Palatinate and finally in North America, where even today ten thousand descendants of those early immigrants live and are often found to be members of Anabaptist-Mennonite churches.

Not until the Enlightenment and after the French Revolution did the repression against the Anabaptists in Europe wane. Influences from Pietism and the revivalist movements in the 18th and 19th centuries allowed the Anabaptist congregations to grow and to find new spiritual life. However, these movements also strengthened the tendency to withdraw from society, which led to an identity of the «quiet in the land». With greater exposure to an increasingly tolerant and pluralistic society in the 20th century, the Anabaptist congregations today are faced with questions of ecclesiastical and theological identity as well.

In Switzerland, one can see a continual presence over the entire time span of Anabaptist-Mennonite existence only in canton Berne. There is one congregation each in the Emmental, in the conglomerations of Berne and Biel as well as in the Neuenburg Jura; in canton Jura there are two congregations, in the region of Basel three, and in the Bernese Jura there are five congregations.

Together, these 14 congregations compose the «Swiss Mennonite Conference» and have a total of approximately 2,500 members; worldwide there are currently a bit more than one million Mennonite Christians on all continents! They are especially numerous outside of Europe in the USA and Canada, in the Democratic Republic of Congo, in India and Indonesia as well as in Paraguay and Mexico.

What Mennonites Believe

Even the Reformed tradition, according to mutual roots in the Reformation, recognizes that there are hardly any differences in central articles of faith. What were then the Anabaptist convictions and behaviors which for centuries both the Swiss government and the church believed they could not tolerate? From today's perspective, we might be wondering: What were the challenges and questions by which an amazingly small number of Anabaptist men and women were able to create such insecurity in their contemporaries?

First of all, the *free church congregation model* of the proponents of believer's baptism questioned the exclusive model of the state church in its narrow symbiotic relationship with the political authority. With the Anabaptist refusal to take oaths, they attested to the fact that they were only willing to swear unconditional obedience to God, but not to earthly authorities.

Secondly, church membership, which was voluntary for the Anabaptists, brought the questions of *freedom of religion and freedom of conscience* to the fore: in the eyes of that early modern society, church membership and regular church attendance were indispensable civic duties. However, for the Anabaptists, both were bound to a personal, voluntary, religious conviction and the readiness to translate this concretely into one's own life.

Thirdly, they were convinced that something of this «*life in Christ*» *would also become outwardly visible* in believers. The sanctifying power of God's Spirit renews the lives of believers in all their frailty. This testimony, this courage for non-conformism, impressed outsiders, but also made them insecure.

Fourthly, *the congregation* played a key role in the practice of this changed-life principle. It is the place of concrete reconciliation and decision-making, the place of encouragement and of correction: in the congregation, people should be able to experience or perceive what good gifts of love and mercy, righteousness and peace God has given to mankind.

An important fifth point is the idea of the *priesthood of all believers* and with that a revaluation and respect of individual believers. Behind this is the conviction that no congregational member has all the gifts, but that each one has been given some gifts. The congregation of Jesus can only exist and develop when all available insights and abilities work together!

Sixthly, Anabaptist communities distinguished themselves time and again by unusual and new forms of *brotherly solidarity* – for instance, through systematic care for the poor within their own congregation, from time to time also for outsiders.

Seventh, something that time and again gave cause for persecution was *the refusal to serve in the military*. Whereas most of the Christian churches unhesitatingly blessed the military campaigns of their governments, here the Anabaptists kept alive something of the recollection of a God who preferred to sacrifice Himself in Jesus Christ rather than to destroy His enemies with power and force.

All of these are matters of concern which the Anabaptist movement has stood for across the centuries in good times and in bad times! Some of these things, in the meantime, have even been lost or have fallen into the background.

Here we cannot be mute concerning the fact that Anabaptist history is full of painful references since many of the matters stated above in a positive light also had drawbacks. Anabaptist courage to be non-conforming has since led to smug know-it-all attitudes, to notorious grumbling and to a retreat from the world into a religious ghetto; the Anabaptist emphasis on «fruits of repentance» and a changed life in Christ has degenerated into a sickening sanctimoniousness and unmerciful legality. In the meantime, some of the matters that embody the legitimately good and biblical spirit have also been adopted by non-Anabaptist churches and groups.

The age of the church as a triumphal majority according to the Constantine pattern seems to have passed – even for the state church. Today, the question of what it means to be «salt and light» as a minority in a pluralistic and individualistic era challenges all churches. This opens new perspectives: dangers as well as opportunities. Anabaptist history and as well as Anabaptist presence know about both.

Concerning Sense and Nonsense of «Reconciliation Events»

For many years, it has been public knowledge that serious dialogue between the Reformed tradition and the Anabaptist-Mennonite tradition has occurred on various levels. It is useful to further reflect theologically the opportunities and limits of such «reconciliation events»: for instance, concerning the motivation of such events, but also concerning the question of whether, and how far, past wrong has consequences even to the present day.

The debates between the Anabaptist movement and the Reformation involved the central issues of being a Christian and of being a church. Both sides have brought forth biblically important emphases, but due to increasing estrangement between them, were understood less and less by the opposite party. Of course, both concepts have been swayed due to a lack of amendment and correction. Today we have the opportunity to learn from each other and to view our respective differences neither as a threat nor as something antagonistic. The following guidelines could be helpful for this process:

1. An essential part of a process of reconciliation is the exploration and an improved knowledge of the history of the two churches.
2. All motivations determining this process – as different

as they may be – deserve attention.

3. A genuine open process of reconciliation can help us to discover anew the strengths and weaknesses of our own tradition and free us to bear a more credible witness.

4. If the process of reconciliation is to make sense, theologically controversial issues must be openly discussed. Reconciliation does not exclude a diversity of opinions.

5. To face the strengths and the weaknesses of our own tradition and to discuss them in mutual respect carries the potential of liberation, healing and renewal.

6. The awareness of the fact that our perception, our experience and our whole life are imperfect (I Cor 13) makes us free to learn from one another, to accept one another in our diversity and in the complementarity resulting from mutual acceptance to live for and with one another.

The Anabaptist Inheritance in Ecumenical Dialogue – A Reformed Perspective

Peter Dettwiler

During my visit to the Eastern Mennonite Seminary in Harrisonburg, VA, in the spring of 2005, one of the professors presented a souvenir to me with the following dedication: «To my brother Peter. This is to thank you for the gift of your presence here this week. May God continue to bless you and others through you. Your Swiss Brethren brother.»

«Swiss Brethren» was the common expression used for the Swiss Anabaptists, while the Dutch Anabaptists on the other hand named themselves *Mennonites* after Menno Simons. Both groups avoided the expressions *Anabaptists* and *Re-baptizers* since at that time they equaled a curse word akin to *heretic*. The fact that a descendant of the «Swiss Brethren» and a Swiss Reformed recognize and respect each other as brothers is one of those small signs of reconciliation. As it has also been recorded in the statement of regret of the Zurich Church of 2004: «We acknowledge the faithful of the Anabaptist tradition as our sisters and brothers and their churches as part of the body of Christ, whose diverse members are united through the Spirit of God.»

The objective of ecumenical endeavors is that we will become a *gift* one to another. In other words, that the richness of the Anabaptist tradition will also become accessible for the Reformed members and that the richness of the Reformed tradition will also become accessible for the Anabaptists and that we will become a blessing to each other.

However, in many respects, an imbalance between the Reformed and Mennonite churches exists. Both churches –

at least in Switzerland – are very different in regard to their size and their geographical expanse, making dialogue more difficult. A further hindrance is our «family history,» which portrays a dark and burdensome chapter lasting some three centuries. An imbalance exists also here: the history of persecution as well as the steps of reconciliation are much more in the Mennonites' consciousness than in that of Reformed members. This deficit is addressed by the Reformed confession of 2004: «It is time to accept the history of the Anabaptist movement as part of our own, to learn from the Anabaptist tradition and to strengthen our mutual testimony through dialogue.»

We are twin sisters! Born from the same reforming movement. Founded on the same foundation, Jesus Christ. Renewed and challenged by the same divine Word of the Bible. But still we have taken different paths; the first-born sister having disowned her twin.

This brings to mind the Old Testament story of Sarai and Hagar. The pregnant maiden flees from the harsh regime of her mistress into the desert, where God meets her: «The Angel of the Lord found her near a spring in the desert. ... And he said: ‹Hagar, servant of Sarai, where have you come from and where are you going?›» (Gen. 16:7ff). Aren't the questions of provenance and destination questions of identity?

There are certain parallels between the story of Sarai and Hagar and our «family history». Both of the half-brothers, Ishmael and Isaac, are Abraham's sons. Mennonites and Reformed are sons and daughters of the Reformation. And just as Hagar was disowned, so were the Anabaptists with their children. In addition, what Ishmael experienced in the desert, the Anabaptist movement also experienced: «God was with the boy.» (Gen. 21:20). And the promise that Hagar received also was fulfilled for the Anabaptists: «I will so increase your descendants that they will be too numerous to count.» (Gen. 16:10). However, God only made the covenant with Isaac and his descendants. He is the «rightful» heir.

Who is the actual heir of the Reformation? Here forming parallels to the biblical account demands great caution. However, it is evident that the Reformed church sees herself as the rightful heir of the (Swiss) Reformation. On the other hand, the Anabaptist tradition claims to have radically fulfilled the Reformed concerns.

Let us return to the decisive question: «Where have you come from and where are you going?» What is our Reformed identity and what is our Anabaptist-Mennonite identity?

One initial comment: For a long time, our churches have defined their identity by their separation from sister churches. The Reformers asserted their identity against the Catholic Church in a negative disassociation. The fact that the Anabaptist identity defined itself in disassociation as well is understandable taking into account the long period of persecution. Today, ecumenical relationships give us the opportunity, in brotherly dialogue, to rediscover anew the riches of our own traditions and therefore to redefine our identity in a positive way.

Identity and Charisma

Each church has a *charisma* that can and should contribute to the building of the entire body of Christ. However, only with mutual synergy and sympathy do these gifts of the spirit develop to their full effect. If churches jealously keep their gifts to themselves, they shrivel or degenerate.[15]

The Reformed church's charisma can be described as the charisma of two poles, concentration and openness. *Concentration* on Christ and the Word. Many Reformed church buildings are simply decorated with a central Bible verse. In this way, everything focuses on this Word, and from this Word, the congregation lives. And from the presence of the risen Lord, wherever two or three are gathered in His Name. The richness of the Reformed church exists just in this simplicity and concentration on the fundamentals of the Christian faith. This concentration frees us to be *open*. To be open to the entire Bible, New and Old Testament, and to actively shape and reshape society. God's kingdom is more important than the church. The Reformed have an unusually distanced relationship with their own church. On the principle of «semper reformanda», continual renewal also includes a diminution of the church as an institution. This ambivalent position over and against one's own church shapes Reformed identity, or rather the uncertainty about one's own identity.

This is why Reformed openness needs to be anchored in concentration on the heart of the Christian faith, if the Reformed church would not lose her identity in turning to the world, which currently and continually threatens the state church in Switzerland.

---

[15] Cf. Oscar Cullmann, *Einheit durch Vielfält* (translation: *Unity through Diversity*), J. C. B. Mohr, Tübingen 1990 (2nd edition), p. 14: Cullmann is convinced «that every Christian confession has an *irrevocable* gift of the spirit, a charisma, that *sustains* it, cares for it, cleanses and deepens it, and should not empty it for the sake of conforming.»

This brief definition of the Reformed charisma is described first here because it may be of help in describing the Anabaptist charisma. In any case, describing the Mennonite identity from the Reformed point of view demands great caution. Since one of the ground rules of ecumenical dialogue is that others not define who we are or have to be, but that each church is allowed to depict itself; that we first listen to each other before we speak about each other. This is why I refer next to a Mennonite voice, namely to an article by *John D. Roth*, which appeared in January 2005 in the American magazine *The Mennonite* under the title: «Give and Take: Thoughts on a ‹Healthy› Mennonite Ecumenism.»

The author mentions the various initiatives for an ecumenical convergence, in particular the reconciliation celebration in Zurich during the summer of 2004 as a preliminary high point, and writes: «These invitations to dialogue have pushed Mennonites to think about their history, faith and practice with a new perspective; and they raise a host of challenging questions about our understanding of Christian ecumenism.»

At the same time, the Mennonites are challenged to gain clarity concerning their understanding of the ecumenical movement. In actual fact, Mennonites are rather reserved about the ecumenical movement, for example in regards to membership in the World Council of Churches. What an encouragement that the person responsible there for the «Decade to Overcome Violence» (2000–2010) is a Mennonite!

John Roth sees four reasons for the caution of the Mennonites towards ecumenical organizations and initiatives: 1. Numerically, they are a tiny church which makes them more careful. 2. The memory of a long history of persecution by the more powerful denominations makes them skeptical. 3. Their concerns for peace and non-violence have kept them at the margins of the religious mainstream. 4. Many fear that ecumenical dialogue could lead to a watering-down of doctrine and a loss of a distinctive identity.

In actuality, Mennonites have long been engaged in ecumenical exchange and have learned much from Christians of other churches and movements. One example cited by John D. Roth is four-part singing, which was «imported» from the Lutherans and previously rejected as a «worldly» practice. True ecumenical encounter therefore leads to the knowledge that God is also at work in other communities. *True ecumenical borrowing* leads to a healthy renewal, according to John D. Roth. This requires, however, the gift of discernment with a posture that is constantly open to a fresh movement of the spirit, but at the same time «resists the impulse to become reeds blowing in the wind with every new religious fad that comes our way». Therefore, Mennonites ask themselves the following questions in ecumenical dialogue: 1. «Does the borrowing help us to embrace a full, rich *understanding of Jesus*?» – «We should embrace insights beyond our tradition that help us to maintain a high view of Jesus in which spiritual concerns and ethical practice are never divorced from each other.» 2. «Does the borrowing promote a view of *the believer's church* as the primary focus of God's saving activity in the world?» – «We should embrace insights beyond our tradition that strengthen our collective worship and elevate the primacy of the gathered church in our mission outreach.» 3. «Finally, does the borrowing help us bear witness to God's *reconciling love* in a world that is deeply broken?» – «We should embrace insights beyond our tradition, which strengthen the commitment to testify in word and deed to God's healing love.»

Summarized according to John D. Roth: «In the Anabaptist-Mennonite tradition, our identity is defined not so much by doctrinal propositions as by a particular religious posture, shaped by the deep roots of our history and our distinctive way of reading the Bible.»

Anabaptist Charisma

What then is the charisma of the Anabaptist tradition? John D. Roth points out three characteristic features to the above question: first of all, to the *integrity* of faith in Jesus Christ, which means the unity of faith and action, of learning and living; secondly, to the life of faith lived out in *community*, which means the church is the community of believers, which in a way is God's «springboard» in this world. Community leadership of the church and community Bible reading are bound together with this. And thirdly, to the witness of *reconciliation* and peace based on the lack of power and the lack of violence of the individual and of the church.

The believer's baptism is the visible sign of this unmistakable identity, namely the expression of the unity of faith and responsible action, witness for the deliberate belonging to the Christian community and the sign of reconciliation of each human being who has died with Christ and lives with Him in the love of their neighbor. In summary, the *charisma of the Anabaptist tradition* could be characterized as follows:

The Anabaptist-Mennonite church has the charisma of integrity, community and reconciliation. These are three aspects of one identity. It is the calling to live the Christian faith in the immutable connection between faith and action, and therefore to live this in community – as a witness to the reconciling love of God.

45

I will close with a small experience I had, once again during my visit in Harrisonburg. While taking leave, one of the hosts came to me and showed me the leather-bound *Martyr's Mirror* that he had inherited from his parents. I knew what significance this costly book had for him personally and for the Anabaptist tradition. «Sometimes», he said, «we are caught in this history of our ancestors. They are our treasure and our burden.» And he asked me to write a dedication in the *Martyr's Mirror*. Only afterwards looking back did I realize what deep symbolism lay in this gesture. A Mennonite opens his *Martyr's Mirror* to a Reformed. We begin to give one another a portion of our treasures. And if we do this, then these costly pearls will begin to shine anew and enrich us both.

The Confession and its Significance

Peter Dettwiler

The confession (statement of regret) from the Reformed church, which was underpinned by the ceremonial appointment of the commemorative plaque for Felix Manz on the bank of the Limmat River, made a broad and positive echo in Anabaptist circles. Reactions on the Reformed side – as far as the confession was even noted – were more reserved. Its clarity bothered some: «We confess that the persecution was, according to our present conviction, a betrayal of the Gospel and that our Reformed forefathers were in error on this issue.»

If the subject here is the «betrayal of the Gospel», then this refers to the *unmerciful* persecution of the Anabaptists, which lasted three centuries in Switzerland and which is also unjustified when taking into account the historical conditions of the Gospel. And furthermore, it refers to the decidedly violent removal of the Anabaptist movement. Heinrich Bullinger, Zwingli's successor and author of the *Second Helvetic Confession*, as well as John Calvin had attempted to justify the use of violence against the Anabaptists – men, women and children – by calling on the Bible and St. Augustine. Individual voices of tolerance towards their brothers in faith went unheard. The Reformed «Inquisition» against the Anabaptist «heretics» and «enemies of the state» remains a dark chapter in the birth of the Reformed church in Switzerland.

It is important, therefore, that the condemnation of the Anabaptists written in the *Second Helvetic Confession* of 1566 be expressly revoked: «We affirm that the judgment against the Anabaptists in the *Second Helvetic Confession*, which discards the teaching of the Anabaptists as unbiblical and refuses any communion with them, is no longer valid for us and that it is now our earnest desire to discover and strengthen our common ties.»

The Lutherans could question the responsibility stemming from this recantation – since the degree of commitment of, for example, the *Second Helvetic Confession* cannot be compared with the *Confessio Augustana* (the Lutheran Augsburg Confession). In fact, the Reformed confessions, already in regards to their multitude, without any hierarchical evaluation, do not hold the weight of the Lutheran tradition of confession, which came to an end in 1580 with the Book of Concord. Furthermore, the Swiss Reformed churches entirely gave up the responsibility of church confession in the 19th century.

This is due to the fact that each catechism and each profession of faith remained secondary and temporary against the holy Scriptures for the Reformed church which was so wholly concentrated on Christ and the Word, as for example Karl Barth underlined in «The Theology of the Reformed Confession» of 1923: «The most important principle is that the teaching of the church be overall and continually grounded in the holy Scriptures, and this is conditioned not necessarily by *unity* of confession, but by the *freedom* of confession of individual churches among themselves and next to each other.»[1]

For Barth, the significance of confession in the Reformed church lays precisely «in its essential insignificance,

---

[1]   Karl Barth, *Die Theologie der Reformierten Bekenntnisschriften* (translation: *The Theology of the Reformed Confessions*), 1923, Karl Barth – Complete Edition, 2nd Academic Works, TVZ 1998, p. 21.

in its evident relativity, in its humanity, in its multiplicity, in its changeability and in its transitoriness.»[2]

Therefore, it is certainly easier for the Reformed churches to amend their own confessions, as it even is required in the preface to the *Second Helvetic Confession*: «Foremost, we attest that we are always fully ready … to give way with thanksgiving to any who teach us a better way from the Word of God and to comply in the Lord, who is to be praised and glorified.»

The Zurich confession of June 26, 2004 follows this Reformed tradition if it complies with this teaching. As with each Reformed confession, its veracity is found first however in its inner coherence and is not based on legitimation through a church authority.

Moreover, the Reformed principle of «semper reformanda» which is so often quoted, requires Reformed members to also submit their relationship with their twin sister, the Anabaptist movement, to this continuous reformation with the readiness to share the Reformed inheritance in ecumenical efforts. Since the long history of Christian division stems from the claim to have administered and realized the biblical or Christian or Reformed inheritance better or purer or even alone. As a matter of fact, we must confess to ourselves today that we have abandoned an important corrective with the violent exodus of the Anabaptists. In this regard, the Zurich Confession of 2004 also states this: «We honor the radical approach of the Anabaptist movement to be the salt of the earth and the light of the world as a free community of committed believers putting into practice the message of the Sermon on the Mount.»

---

[2]   Ibid., p. 63.

This respect is the basis for an ecumenical dialogue, which leads to the realization that the specific charisma that God has entrusted to each church will no longer be mis-used to divide, but rather to bring about mutual enrichment and fulfillment.

New Horizons

John Sharp: The Story Now Has a New Ending

When Mennonites and Amish from rural Pennsylvania or Ohio have encountered the rolling hills of the Swiss Emmental, they have often exclaimed with a sense of awe: «I feel so at home here.» I told the Zurich conference that now, after enjoying the generosity and hospitality of the Reformed church: «We will now also feel at home in Zurich.»

And that changes how I will tell the story. As usual, I will tell the story of the Zurich Reformation fueled by Zwingli's preaching in the Grossmünster; the first believer's baptism on Neustadt Gasse within the shadow of the cathedral; the martyrdom of Felix Manz in the icy waters of the Limmat River; the stubborn resistance of Hans Landis, who told the Zurich authorities they had no right to seize his property or expel him from the canton because «the earth is the Lord's» and not theirs.

Now as I stand on the west bank of the Limmat under the Lindenhof, I will read the text of the new stone tablet: «From a fishing platform here in the middle of the Limmat Felix Manz and five other Anabaptists were drowned between 1527 and 1532, during the time of the Reformation. The last Anabaptist to be executed in Zurich was Hans Landis in 1614.»

This, I will say, is the new ending to the story. The Zurich persecutors, who for centuries had wished to forget this story but are now choosing to remember it, placed this marker here. They have acknowledged their «historic sin» and consider the persecution «a betrayal of the gospel». They have asked for our forgiveness.

They and we are «branches of the one and the same bough of the great Christian tree». We are called to work together as God's reconciling ministers «in small things and great ones». Given this common charge, we can now feel at home in Zurich.

Photo Three: John E. Sharp (right) receiving a present from Ruedi Reich at the inauguration of the memorial June 26, 2004.

Franklin Yoder: Too Late for an Apology?

I went to Zurich not certain of what to expect. Personally, I had never anguished over the fact that the Reformed church had played a major part in Felix Manz's execution. I harbored no ill-will toward people who call themselves Reformed, and I was not sure how to be reconciled to someone who had done me no wrong. But as I attended the various events, I found the experience to be fulfilling and my perspective broadened and changed.

Two things impressed me. First, being in Zurich and seeing the church and its setting deepened my understanding of how and why the events of 1525 led to Manz's death. There is no substitute for being at the place where history has been made, and this was true for me.

An exhibit inside the Grossmünster told the story of Heinrich Bullinger, and it helped explain why the Reformers saw people such as Manz as serious threats.

Secondly, even though I did not feel a compelling need to be reconciled to the Reformed Church of Zurich, I found the event to be moving. In a sense, the appropriate time for this to happen was many years earlier. Nonetheless, the words I heard reminded me that wrongs can be addressed years later and can bring a sense of healing.

As I watched and listened, I decided there can be value in such requests. I was especially impressed with the expressions of regret and statements of hope offered by representatives of the Reformed church. They were taking their history seriously, and by not ignoring this aspect of their past they showed an honesty and sense of responsibility that I found refreshing and uplifting. The Reformed church may have received the greatest benefit from this time, because asking for forgiveness is more difficult and perhaps more meaningful than accepting forgiveness.

We are always quick to celebrate our triumphs and claim them as our own, but too often we are less willing to acknowledge our shortcomings and failures.

Part of me wondered if we as Anabaptists should also have apologized for the actions of our spiritual ancestors. Our own histories have mostly overlooked the chaos and disruption our Anabaptist forebears brought to the society in which they lived. I do believe that killing the Anabaptists was wrong, but I also see how their actions were at times extreme and unhelpful. There is ample evidence that some early Anabaptists operated with a sense of righteous indignation, stubbornness and arrogance that is characteristic of people who believe they alone have an insight into God's will. There are usually two sides to every story, and that is the side of our history that we speak of infrequently, if at all.

Dan Nighswander: Zurich Reflections

I believe that this act of reconciliation has immediate and future significance for Mennonites and the various expressions of the Reformed church (Christian Reformed, Presbyterian, United, etc.) in Canada and other countries as well as in Switzerland. Only by facing up to the facts of the past can the spiritual descendants of Zwingli and the spiritual descendants of Felix Manz stand shoulder-to-shoulder as reconciled siblings in the family of Christ. Events like this gathering in Zurich enable and force us to stop seeing ourselves either as sectarian victims of persecution or as more favored by God because of the martyrdom of some of our forebears.

But reconciliation requires more than one meeting, and there are still questions to be answered. Some of the questions have already begun to be discussed in meetings between the Reformed churches and Anabaptist churches in 1983 and 1989. These previous meetings have called for local congregations of our two traditions to get acquainted and to find ways to serve Christ together.

John Rempel: Live Out the Reconciliation

The event took place in the Grossmünster, the mother church of both Reformed and Anabaptist Christianity in Switzerland. It was here that Zwingli preached the liberating message of the Bible. It was from Zwingli's pulpit that Larry Miller, executive secretary of the Mennonite World Conference, preached a message of healing and challenge. It was from the baptismal font that the president of the cantonal church declared with evident emotion that the Reformed had contradicted their own understanding of the gospel by using coercion in matters of faith.

What should we make of this extraordinary gesture? I came away with enormous gratitude, and with a lingering sense of unfinished ecumenical business. I found it remarkable that an institution of power had asked for forgiveness. Our Reformed hosts put an aspect of their own history into question. And they did so in the year dedicated to the accomplishments of Zwingli's successor, Heinrich Bullinger.

An ancient wound is now healed and a new era has begun. Now our calling is to live out the reconciliation the Holy Spirit has worked in us.

While I was in Zurich I made it a point to converse with as many Reformed ministers as possible. They were all gracious, receptive and inquisitive about our ways. But they were also committed to the notion of a state church as firmly as in the 16th century. A minister committed to reaching unchurched people confided his discouragement to me. Later in the conversation I suggested that part of the problem in making the gospel appealing might be the union of church and state. He was shocked. He couldn't imagine the church surviving without the financial and administrative support of the state.

Regarding the freedom of the church from the state, nothing seemed to have changed. Our task now is to imitate the spirit of repentance and repent of our own sins. And when we have become good at that there might come a day when we can engage our Swiss friends in more dialogue about our contrary understandings of the church.

Jon M. Ebersole: Healing is Possible

When I was a child I learned two things simultaneously about Switzerland, before I was able to find it on a map. First, that my family left Switzerland long ago, and second, that they left because the Swiss were tying up the leaders of our church and drowning them in the Limmat River.

That was 480 years ago now. Like several hundred thousand other Mennonites and Amish, scattered around the globe, I grew up with a book called the *Martyr's Mirror* which recorded these deaths and built part of our identity.

Then two summers ago, the Zurich City Council and the Reformed Church of Zurich, formally apologized to the Amish and Mennonites. I was at the event. It took place on the bank of the Limmat River. I can tell you that I felt a burden lifted that I had not been completely aware of. At the same time, it felt a bit ridiculous. I grew up in the American suburbs, in peace, security and middle class materialism. «Do we really need to do this?» wrote one Mennonite author last year. The short answer is «yes». Carolyn Yoder writes that collective trauma require collective healing processes before we can put these events behind us, so that we are no longer driven by the pain handed down to us from our ancestors. The message of this little story is that healing is possible, thank God healing is possible. Trust can be restored.

Reformed Perspectives: Why Seek Dialogue with the Anabaptists?

Michael Baumann

The question «Why seek dialogue with the Anabaptists?» might appear well neigh insulting, certainly in a little volume that begins with a deep and earnest confession. This confession names the Reformed church's long and disastrous persecution of Anabaptists and is the expression of a church community's new – and newly strengthened – sense of shame at the sight of the cases of injustices that were once perpetrated on Anabaptists.

The naming of historical injustice is essential. It is particularly necessary for a church to realize that it is, as an institution, always an earthly community and as such flawed and susceptible to error. To practice such a form of self-restraint is a protection against arrogance and against the many falsifications of the true kingdom of God.

The failures of the past can, at least in limited form, suggest some of the things which cannot be ignored if one is to avoid repeating the same mistakes in the future.

However, beyond this we need to ask what more specific lessons the Reformed churches can learn from a more extended dialogue with Anabaptist churches and communities. The following points are intended to stimulate more thought in this direction.

Facing Suffering

The Reformed churches of Switzerland stand in a tradition of intricate intertwinement with their own history and society. This holds as much for the history of their growth and their historical influence on politics, culture and society as for their sorry history of the oppression and marginalization of those who, at various times, did not fit into some framework of what was, or was supposed to be, normative. Here, churches were guilty of causing suffering – which is all the more tragic since, often enough, they too found themselves in the role of the victims who were forced to bear the weight of suffering. Apparently, both the experience and the perpetration of suffering belong to the foundations of Reformed history.

Given the message of Christ's own suffering it is important to give words to the suffering – whether caused or sustained – of Christian communities. Here, the remembrance of Christ's own suffering can serve as a guiding principle. Such a principle cannot be understood as the path of cheap grace; on the contrary, the remembrance of Christ's suffering helps us not to repress suffering but to better understand its meaning.

What does this teach us in view of a coming to terms with the history of the relations between the Reformed churches and the Anabaptist communities?

Toward the Anabaptist communities, we are posed with the task of extending an open hand. To beg forgiveness after centuries of neglect may seem trite, perhaps even cynical. However, the appeal of this extended hand goes beyond a mere apology by indicating a willingness to listen to the voice and opinions of sister churches that have been marginalized for far too long. This listening should take place in the shared confession of the risen Lord, who promised, through his own suffering, a way to life outside of earthly oppositions and hierarchies of power. This helps us to keep the dialogue from remaining at a level of superficial friendliness, entering instead into a form characterized by true reciprocal interest and an active desire to find new ways of thinking about and understanding the meaning of baptism

Taking the Questions Seriously

The faith and practice of the Anabaptists called an apparently obvious tradition into question. To question the baptism of children implied considerably more than a debate about the most genuine form of the rite described in the New Testament.

Behind this stand questions about the possibility of experiencing and remembering the proximity of God and about vital Christian community.

One could in a sense think of the Anabaptist churches as an «incarnated» objection to the teaching and practice of Reformed theology. That, from the very beginning of the Reformation, an offshoot should have grown out of the specifically Reformed tradition – and that it should have survived every form of repression to produce its own fruits and traditions of faith should serve both as an indication and a constant warning to question our own understanding of baptism and to familiarize ourselves with the motivations and convictions of the Anabaptist tradition.

At the very least, this contrast to the other branch of Reformation churches places on the Reformed position the onus of continuously questioning its legitimacy – to reach a new, more thoughtful kind of reassurance.

Rethinking Baptism

Dialogue with the Anabaptists challenges Reformed Christians to reassess and formulate their own convictions about baptism. This cannot take place in the context of an irrefragable insistence on long-standing practice but in the willingness to question one's own positions in true dialogue.

While it may well be impossible to reach a final answer about proper baptismal practice, it is at least possible to reach some degree of certainty about what baptism is meant to be, to achieve and to represent. Exchanges with Anabaptist churches have shown that both positions hold to an underlying conviction that God's grace is always precedent to baptism. However, it is still necessary to come to terms with questions about the consequences of each form of baptismal practice.

Moreover, taking each others' differing ways of understanding of baptism seriously requires that churches present baptism to their own church members in a new fashion. Reformed churches make an effort to celebrate baptism not simply as a family celebration but to emphasize its meaning for Christian life. Further steps could well follow. There is certainly no reason to risk ecumenical achievements, nor any question that baptism is a one-time, sacramental act. However, the consciousness that one enters membership in a Christian church *through* baptism could certainly be deepened.

Venturing New Steps

What does baptism mean to us and how can it be cultivated? Both – indeed, all – Christian churches agree that baptism marks the unshakable entrance of human beings into God's presence – their initiation into a relationship with God. Moreover, Reformed churches agree that what takes place in the sacrament must find expression in a biographical reality that can be experienced and remembered. There are several ways of making this possible, including the task of clarification at the age of confirmation, celebrations of baptismal remembrance for (young) adults or grownups, a visible baptismal register in churches, baptismal services with children, alternative baptismal celebrations with youth and the integration of baptism in Christian education. Moreover, experimental forms like celebrating the anniversaries of baptisms or confirmations, holding special services for baptismal re-affirmation or taking up baptism in pastoral care and counseling should all be attempted – and have, in fact, already been successfully implemented.

The Reformed church should not miss the chance to highlight baptism as a central topic also in liturgy, pastoral care, spiritual biography and Christian education. Only in so doing can the church finally – and creatively – begin to address a 500-year-old objection and put it to work for her well-being.

Second Part

Steps to Reconciliation

Documents of the Conference
«The Reformation and the Anabaptists»
June 26, 2004, Zurich, Switzerland

«They too are Reformed»

Stephan Landis

The conference «The Reformation and the Anabaptists» facing the history of alienation and persecution was on the one hand about gestures of reconciliation, and on the other hand about discussions regarding similarities and differences.

«We are therefore not Anabaptists and do not have anything in common with them», Bullinger stated in the *Second Helvetic Confession* of 1566.

«Here Heinrich Bullinger errs historically and theologically», commented Ruedi Reich, Church Council President of the Evangelical-Reformed Church of the Canton of Zurich, looking at a long history of alienation and persecution for which Bullinger and the Reformed churches all carry the responsibility.

In conjunction with this a picture, irritating and moving all at the same time: high above the chancel staircase in the Grossmünster Church hangs the portrait of the Reformer Bullinger preaching as a part of the current Bullinger exhibit. Located beneath this portrait, a Mennonite ad-hoc choir comes together and sings an old hymn from a tradition to which the Anabaptists have held on unwaveringly throughout centuries of oppression.

Approximately 300 visitors, many of them Mennonites from Switzerland, Europe and overseas, have taken part in the conference, which the Zurich Reformed Church organized within the framework of the Bullinger Jubilee Year. Among the guests from overseas was even a descendent of Hans Landis, who was the last of seven Zurich Anabaptist leaders to be executed in 1614.

Along with these signs, «Steps to Reconciliation» formed a main focus of the conference. These were not the first steps; since the dismantling of state repression in the wake of the Enlightenment and Pietism, there have been theological and ecumenical contacts with Anabaptists from time to time.

Photo Four: Mennonite ad-hoc choir in Zurich's Grossmünster.

Two symbolic gestures stood in the foreground on June 26, 2004: on the one hand, a confession of the Evangelical-Reformed Church of the Canton Zurich, presented by Ruedi Reich in the framework of a communal worship service in the Grossmünster: «We confess that the persecution was, according to our present conviction, a betrayal of the Gospel and that our Reformed forefathers were in error on this issue.» On behalf of the Swiss Mennonite Conference, Ernest Geiser, President of the Council of Elders of that body, expressed thanks saying: «We receive your confession with a forgiving attitude.» In current times, for the Swiss

Mennonites, «there is no longer any church for us to oppose, and you no longer have any believers to re-integrate by force». The Mennonites show a desire for a long-lasting dialogue as well.

As a second gesture of reconciliation in the framework of the conference, a commemorative plaque was unveiled at the site where Felix Manz, as the first Anabaptist, was drowned in the Limmat River in 1527. The first plan for such a plaque fell flat in 1952 after the Zurich City Council objected. On Saturday, Robert Neukomm, representing the current city government, thought that the refusal of his predecessors would hardly be comprehensible today. Like Ruedi Reich, who addressed the Mennonites for a second time on that occasion, Neukomm also asked for forgiveness for the execution of the seven Anabaptist leaders and additionally for the oppression and expulsion of the Anabaptist congregations.

The fact that such gestures of reconciliation cannot clear away all reservations in one fell swoop became clear in Zurich in that the attendees did not share in communion during the worship service – taking into consideration objections of North American guests. For this reason, it was particularly important on the Zurich conference to have moments of critical contextual analysis of the position of the opposition (and through that also of one's own).

Therefore, Hanspeter Jecker, Professor at the Bienenberg Mennonite Theological Seminary, formulated theses concerning the strengths and weaknesses of the Anabaptist movement as a critical inquiry to his own and to the Reformed traditions. As historical strengths, he cited the free church congregational model against the often deficient symbiotic relationship between the state church and the state; voluntary church membership as the impulse towards freedom of religion and conscience; the courage to be nonconformist as a conviction that life in Christ should also become visible to the outside; the key roles of the congregation as a place of concrete reconciliation and decision-making; the increased value of individual church members encapsulated in the idea of the priesthood of all believers; new forms of solidarity and the refusal of military service versus the uncritical blessing by some state churches for military actions. On the other hand, Jecker self-critically mentioned an Anabaptist tendency to know-it-all attitudes and sanctimoniousness, to a retreat from the world into a religious ghetto and to a traumatized spirit of human fear as the flip side of the coin to the strengths listed above.[1]

Church Council President Ruedi Reich – in addition to dangers such as that of non-commitment – named special opportunities and strengths of the state church: for example the church presence in hospitals and prisons, but also in train stations and airports, or the unity that the state church could maintain in the 19th century whilst free churches split multiple times. At the same time, the church separated itself from all of the confessions and retained only the «Gospel of Jesus Christ» as its foundation, which we must bring into our own congregation over and over again. In addition, Reich acknowledged the ecumenical movement, in particular with the Catholic Church, the equal participation of women in the state church, the charitable tradition of the Reformation and the ongoing shaping of the church by the religio-social movement so that social issues remain a main concern for the church.

Pierre Bühler, Professor for Systematic Theology and originally from an Anabaptist family in the Bernese Jura, used theses to demonstrate areas for a fruitful discussion

---

[1]   Cf. pp. 34–37, «What Mennonites Believe».

between Anabaptists and Reformed under the title «State Church or Confessing Church?»[2] The Reformed church, living out of the tradition of the majority church, currently finds itself increasingly confronted with the difficulties of a minority church, whereby the Anabaptist church, perceiving themselves traditionally as a minority church, must increasingly stand up to the challenges of a majority church – which it itself will never be.

For Bühler, this shows itself, for example, in the old «reason for division», concerning the question of adult and child baptism: today the Reformed church is rediscovering adult baptism as a sign of a binding responsibility for the faith. The Anabaptists, on the other hand, are dealing with the possibility of consecration of infants, in order to embed family life in the modern world in the assurance of the love of God.

A follow-up podium discussion showed two further, more virulent points, which Bühler cited: the first being the membership issue. The formal regulation by the state church, in extreme cases only through church taxation, allows the differentiation between the visible and the invisible church, but brings the danger of non-commitment with it. On the other hand, membership based on voluntary involvement can also turn a free-will decision into an obligation.

A second problem which led to an animated discussion at the event, was the issue of the church's relationship to the general public and to the world. According to Bühler, the Anabaptist movement wanted to express contrast to the world, but through this fell into the danger of favoring a withdrawal from it. However, the state church sees itself as

---

[2]   Cf. theses on pp. 85–87.

being closely bound to the world and society, but can easily be suspected of secularization. For Ruedi Reich it is «simply a fact that we are involved in the world.» This is not a question of church structure. Today, the degree of limitation crosses church forms: state churches, which are scolded because of their connection with the state, are often more critical than free churches.

The Mennonite pastor Ernest Geiser noted a tendency in the Anabaptists to take on more societal responsibility than previously; in conjunction with this, Bühler noted a certain weariness in the Reformed church in acting as the watchman for state and society. Such discussions between Anabaptists and Reformed remained focused on the emphasis on our common ground during the entire Zurich conference. The historian Urs B. Leu underlined the initial closeness of the Anabaptists to Zwingli; Larry Miller, General Secretary of the Mennonite World Conference, reminded us how much the Anabaptists would have learned from Reformed theologians such as Barth, Moltmann or Lukas Vischer; Ruedi Reich encouraged us to see our tradition of many voices not just as a theological problem. Setri Nyomi, General Secretary of the World Alliance of Reformed Churches, bringing in an African church point of view which does not bear the weight of such a difficult history, emphasized the opportunities of an agreement on a local level. And in a reconciliatory statement, Thomas Wipf, Council President of the Federation of Swiss Protestant Churches, brought to a point the relationship of the Reformed to the Anabaptist «radical Reformation» with which his parents explained to him the nature of a Mennonite host: «They too are Reformed, but simply a bit more Reformed than we are.»

The New City

Sermon delivered by Larry Miller, General Secretary of the Mennonite World Conference, on the Grossmünster pulpit, June 26, 2004.

«Jerusalem shall be inhabited like villages without walls, because of the multitude of people and animals. For I will be a wall of fire all around it, says the LORD, and I will be the Glory within it.»
(Zechariah, 2:4b–5)

«You are the salt of the earth. ... You are the light of the world. A city built on a hill cannot be hid. No one after lighting a lamp puts it under the bushel basket, but on the lampstand, and it gives light to all in the house. In the same way, let your light shine before others, so that they may see your good works and give glory to your Father in heaven.» (Matthew 5:13–16)

A Tale of Two Cities

The history that began in this very place nearly five centuries ago, with one group of people gathered around one Bible, listening to one man (Zwingli) preaching daily from the Gospel of Matthew has resulted in at least two communities, two identities, and two traditions too often in opposition to each other.

The Scripture passages chosen for us today offer two images of God's city, two parables of God's people, each one symbolizing one of our traditions. The Zechariah passage (2:5–9, or 2:1–5) can represent a Reformed tradition of the church as state-church or a peoples' church, as community open to all citizens without exception while giving allegiance to the Lord. The second (Mt. 5:13–16) is typical of Anabaptist-related traditions of the church as the community of disciples following Jesus in life daily, separated from the world while witnessing to it.

Yet, when held up as mirrors to our own history and identity, the passages we select as self-characteristic can function as texts of self-condemnation, or at least as calls to confession.

Photo Five: Larry Miller preaching from the pulpit in the Grossmünster June 26, 2004.

A City Open to the World?

Zechariah addresses an appeal to those still living in exile, exhorting them to return to the city whose new conditions he envisions. This city will be an open city, a city for exiles, a city for a great multitude of people and other creatures. It will be a city that needs no walls for security and cohesion because the Lord himself will be present to protect and to provide. «I will be a wall of fire all around it, says the Lord, and I will be the glory within it.»

From a 16th century Anabaptist point of view, this passage must have seemed more like a «condemnation» of the Reformed church's practice of state-church theology than the model for it. For Felix Manz and his siblings in the faith, Zurich or its church was finally not an open city, not a new Jerusalem, not a place of justice and peace to which they or a multitude of others could return from exile. They did not have the impression that Zurich authorities were depending only on the presence of the Lord for the city's protection, provision and glory. This city must have felt to them like a closed city, one in which they were declared foreign, one from which they were exiled outside the high wall or into dark death in the waters of the Limmat.

A City on a Hill: Light to the World?

In Matthew, Jesus addresses an appeal to those who have voluntarily exiled themselves from established society in order to follow him. He sets before them the vision of a new city, a new society, a new community that is not «of the world» yet fully «in the world». And not only will this city be fully in the world. It will be there as «salt and light». It will be there in such way that no one can avoid tasting it or seeing it, how it lives, whom it follows, on whom it depends for protection and provision, whom it glorifies. «A city built on a hill *cannot* be hid. ... Let your light shine before others, so that they may see your good works and give glory to your Father in heaven.»

For some of us who claim the Anabaptist tradition as our own, these words of Jesus resonate more like a «condemnation» of significant parts of our history than their source of inspiration. Several of the earliest radical reformers, including Felix Manz, no doubt envisioned large-scale transformation of society or at least vigorous witness to it through communities of believers living in its midst. But after persistent persecution, many found themselves sooner or later in tightly knit, separatist communities, without significant prophetic or evangelizing fervor. Many of us have voluntarily stayed there, marginalized, little more than a footnote in church history or, more recently, found relief in some form of accommodation to host societies. After lighting the lamp, we hid it under the bushel where it neither illuminates good works nor provokes offerings of glory to God.

Fortunately, this tale of two cities – the open city inhabited by the Lord and the city set on a hill glorifying God – reminds us not only of our limits. It also points to gifts we have received and can offer one another, and others. The Bible not only calls us to confession. It also calls us to share God-given gifts in the body of Christ and beyond.

Sharing Gifts
The Reformed Call to an Open Community

Today, in the spirit of Zechariah, you – Reformed Christians – open your city and the church in it not only to the daughters and sons of those put to death or exiled in the 16th century and later. More importantly, you open yourselves to another look at the convictions those exiles incarnated. Today, you take steps toward right remembering, toward right relations, toward fuller communion with former adversaries. Today, you demonstrate your openness to depend on God for protection and provision. You manifest your faith that the Lord will be the wall of fire around you and the glorious presence in your midst. This is a precious gift and a clear message to the Anabaptist-related community worldwide, indeed to the whole ecumenical church.

May we be ready to receive your gifts! May we be ready to receive not only your humility and generosity this day but also, more fundamentally, the God-given elements in your experience, tradition, identity and imagination of the open city.

Growing up in a Mennonite church and studying in Mennonite educational institutions, I learned early on that «Jesus is Lord.» But I attribute the deep realization that Jesus is Lord of history and of creation – of the whole world and all that is within it – to the witness of Reformed Christians. My brand of Mennonite theology focused on the lordship of Christ over the church, over the new city set on a hill.

Reformed dialogue partners lifted up Jesus as Lord of all, not only of the church but of the whole world and everything in it. The church is called to shape society as much as possible according to God's will, they said. If the issue of peace is adequately to be addressed, they added, looking Mennonites straight in the eye, the Gospel must be related not only to questions of war and military affairs, but also to all that which constitutes life in the institutions of civilization that were intended to preserve and enhance human life – families, economic and technological systems, patterns cultural and political. After all, it was a theology of Reformed orientation that was most able to give guidance and language to the resistance of Protestants to Hitler, partly in the form of a «Confessing Church». Since then, several generations of Mennonites have received much from Reformed teachers and partners: from Karl Barth, André Trocmé, Jacques Ellul, Jürgen Moltmann, Milan

Opocensky, Lukas Vischer, to name only a few. Thank you for this gift.

Sharing Gifts
The Anabaptist Call to be a City on a Hill

It may be simpler to see what others can give us than what we can give them.

When other Christians look at today's descendants of Anabaptists, they typically see several gifts. When they look at Amish, they see the gift of simplicity. When they look at Hutterites, they see the gift of economic sharing. When they look at Mennonites, they see the gift of peacemaking. Each of these gifts does have something to do with living as a free church, as a believer's church, as a peace church, as a community of disciples living as salt and light in the world.

In a book named «Body Politics, Five Practices of the Christian Community Before the Watching World», the most influential Mennonite theologian of the 20th century, John Howard Yoder, names five components of the life in the city built on a hill which give light if appropriately extended into the world.

Binding and loosing (Mt. 18:15ff.), known also as the «Rule of Christ», a biblical process of reconciliation and moral discernment.

Breaking bread together, also called the «Lord's Supper» and the «Eucharist», understood as including or implying economic sharing among the members of the community of believers.

Baptism practiced as entry into a community where social, ethnic and national categories and hierarchies no longer apply or separate.

Living the *fullness of Christ* in which every member of the community – and not only the pastor or preacher – has a distinctly identifiable, divinely validated and communitarian empowered role.

Applying the *Rule of Paul* (I Cor. 14), that is, making decisions through a process in which every church member may be inspired by the Spirit to speak, then validating that word by the consensus of the entire group.

Are these gifts twenty-first century Anabaptists have to offer to other Christians and the world? Perhaps sometimes, when we actually practice what we preach. But in any case, I expect that Reformed Christians will be surprised to hear these practices called typically «Anabaptist.» After all, most of them are at least partly rooted also in earliest Reformed convictions or theology. And their rediscovery by 20th century Anabaptist historians and theologians is rooted in dialogue with 20th century Reformed historians and theologians. Even the gifts we may have to offer you are in some sense gifts you have already given to us!

Making All Things New

Our traditions are important to us. They are important to us because we believe them to be vehicles of truth and, perhaps even more, because they are places of belonging: they are *our* traditions, *our* identities, *our* places of belonging. Shortly after the Mennonite World Conference began the dialogue with the Catholic Church under the theme «Towards a Healing of Memories». I received an anonymous letter leveling the charge that we were «betraying the blood of the martyrs». To offer confession, to respond to confession, to take steps toward reconciliation and then beyond reconciliation into fuller unity can feel like betrayal of truth and loss of identity.

But these fears assume that identity is something static and its preservation contingent on defending «our» tradition against «other» traditions. Yet the Lord is the wall of fire around us and the glory in our midst. We who have confessed our faith belong neither to ourselves nor to our traditions – each of which contain distortions. We belong to Jesus Christ and to the one body of Christ in whom «everything becomes new».

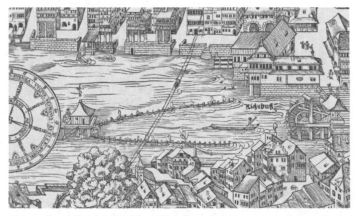

Photo Six: City of Zurich 1576. Detail from a map drawn by Jos Murer with the fisher hut in the middle of the Limmat River. From the platform the Anabaptists were drowned.

There is, after all, an ultimate biblical vision of the new city, one no doubt inspired by and fulfilling the earlier visions of Zechariah and Jesus.

«Then I saw a new heaven and a new earth ... and I saw the holy city, the new Jerusalem, coming down out of heaven from God ... I saw no temple in the city, for its temple is the Lord God the Almighty and the Lamb. And this city has no need of sun or moon to shine on

it, for the glory of God is its light, and its lamp is the Lamb. The nations will walk by its light, and the kings of the earth will bring their glory into it. Its gates will never be shut by day – and there will be no night there. People will bring into it the glory and the honor of the nations.» (Rev. 21:1–2, 22–27).

This new city is our common horizon and our shared future. But before we enter it, while continuing to live together in exile, we have many more steps to take along the path re-opened here today.

Twenty years ago, after sharing in a public service of confession and communion in this cathedral, followed by a consultation in Strasbourg, the World Alliance of Reformed Churches and the Mennonite World Conference wrote a message and a study booklet for member churches worldwide:

«The time has indeed come», they said, «for us to look afresh at our relationship to each other and to our common calling to follow Christ in the church and in the world. It is our hope that this booklet will prompt and facilitate renewed conversation in our worldwide fellowships on these matters. Theological and practical considerations suggest that the conversation begin at the local level.» (pp. 7–8).

«MWC and WARC would like to be informed of local and regional initiatives. In approximately two years we will report the development and results of these conversations. At that time also, we will consider appropriate next steps.» (p. 2).

There was little response to the call issued 20 years ago. There was nothing to report after two years, and not much more after two decades. Meeting in occasional special events to seek and extend forgiveness is simpler than sustained dialogue and cooperation, not to mention the long and hard work of growing into unity in the one body of Christ. So together we, the World Alliance of Reformed

Churches and the Mennonite World Conference, announce our hope that the events of this day in Zurich and future dialogue in Switzerland will serve as a catalyst and example to Mennonites, Amish, Hutterites and Reformed world-wide. Where we encounter one another with a common commitment to Scripture and with openness to mutual correction and sharing, we can expect to be led by the Spirit beyond our brokenness into God's new city.

Statement of Regret

This confession was read by Ruedi Reich, President of the Council of the Evangelical-Reformed Church of the Canton of Zurich, in the Grossmünster, June 26, 2004.

The Reformed churches and the Anabaptist movement are all essentially branches on one and the same bough of the great Christian tree. Both are offspring of the Reformation. Right from the start however they went their separate ways, so that a tragic rift ran through the Zurich Reformation, painful traces of which are discernable to this day. Executions, persecution and expulsions were carried out to eliminate the Anabaptist movement. Yet it has survived and is still flourishing today. The descendants of those early Anabaptists are a living testimony to this.

The persecuted do not forget their history; the persecutors by contrast would prefer to do so. We – representatives of the Reformed State Church of the Canton of Zurich – acknowledge that our church has largely suppressed the story of the persecution of the Anabaptists.

We confess that the persecution was, according to our present conviction, a betrayal of the Gospel and that our Reformed forefathers were in error on this issue.

We affirm that the judgment against the Anabaptists in the *Second Helvetic Confession,* which discards the teaching of the Anabaptists as unbiblical and refuses any communion with them, is no longer valid for us and that it is now our earnest desire to discover and strengthen our common ties.

We acknowledge the faithful of the Anabaptist tradition as our sisters and brothers and their churches as part of the body of Christ, whose diverse members are united through the Spirit of God.

We honor the radical approach of the Anabaptist movement to be the salt of the earth and the light of the world as a free community of committed believers putting into practice the message of the Sermon on the Mount.

It is time to accept the history of the Anabaptist movement as part of our own, to learn from the Anabaptist tradition and to strengthen our mutual testimony through dialogue.

Following the example of our Reformed tradition,
we confess:

We do not belong to ourselves. We belong to Jesus Christ who calls us to follow him and to be reconciled with those brothers and sisters who have any just reasons to reproach us.

We do not belong to ourselves. We belong to Jesus Christ who reconciles us with God through his death on the cross and has committed to us the ministry of reconciliation.

We do not belong to ourselves. We belong to Jesus Christ who tore down the wall of enmity and united people near and far in one body.

Mennonite Response

Dear members of the Reformed Church of Zurich, our brothers and sisters in Christ

We are very touched to have been invited to prepare and live out this day with you. Already in 1925 and in 1952, other international Mennonite representatives were officially welcomed here in this place which represents a very significant moment at the beginning of our history. Though issuing from the same source in the Reformation, Anabaptism has been marked by the breaking off and rejection of the accents of a radical theology and the «following» of Christ. Persecution, in Zurich and in other places, provoked the scattering of the Anabaptists in many other countries where our way of understanding were lived out and tested in many different situations.

As of today, Swiss Mennonites as such are no longer present in the region around Zurich. Throughout the last few centuries, we have been influenced in different ways. Having been pushed to the side, we have become used to – and even find some satisfaction in – being cut off from the world and society. We confess that the reality of our communities do not always correspond to our interpretation of the Gospel; we can find conformism, atrophy, withdrawal and pride there.

History may designate us as victims and could incite us to find satisfaction in that. However, those here among you today, descendants of those Anabaptists persecuted in the past, no longer feel as victims. We do not ask for material retribution for the past: that would seem to us to be contrary to the Spirit of the Gospel. But the fact that you recognize the difficult points of your history in relation to ours helps us to see ourselves and to meet you differently.

We thank you therefore for your statement and wish to accept it in a spirit of forgiveness.

For many years now, and in many places, many opportunities for collaboration between members of Reformed and Mennonite churches have demonstrated a common will to overcome our old conflicts and to live out our belonging to the same body of Christ. This is why it is sometimes embarrassing for us to be once again asked for forgiveness. Maybe it is a sign that it is the moment for all of us to revisit our past, with the help of the Holy Spirit? There is no longer any church for us to oppose, and you no longer have any believers to re-integrate by force. We maintain however strong convictions, which are often shared by other free church movements issued from successive revivals, in particular to that which pertains to more ethical and ecclesiological questions, that we would like to see more widely shared throughout the body of Christ. And we would like to engage in a longer dialogue concerning our church and theological traditions in order to reinforce our common witness to Jesus Christ and his Gospel.

The 26th of June 2004 will remain an important step forward on the road of reconciliation. The plaque that will be unveiled today in this city of Zurich attests that actions have been taken with determination. We feel concerned by your words and deeds and we want to express our gratitude. Dear brothers and sisters of the Reformed Church of Zurich, may God bless you and give you his grace and his peace!

Swiss Mennonite Conference

State Church or Confessing Church?
11 Theses

Pierre Bühler

The author grew up in the Sonnenberg Mennonite Church (in the Bernese Jura). The decision to study theology at university provoked a process of letting go: he feels more Reformed from the perspective of church membership and rather Lutheran regarding theological orientation. However, he never radically broke from his Anabaptist heritage, but has remained in lively conversation with these churches' representatives. The tension between the Anabaptist and Reformed inheritance has permanently marked him. This is why, on the occasion of the June 26, 2004 conference, he wanted to explicitly discuss this specific theme – this tension – as a tension between two ecclesiastical models which are closer to each other in current times than one might think. The following theses were presented and elaborated upon in a workshop, then they were discussed in a dialogue with the participants.

1. The Anabaptist movement and the Reformed church developed from the *common root* of the Reformation; after having lived long in opposition to one another or next to each other, they now are allowed to communicate more with each other.

2. Through this dialogue, one church is fruitfully challenged by the other, since both find themselves facing new responsibilities by which both are challenged to introspection.

3. This does not involve leveling out all *differences*, but allowing them to have a constructive effect; reconciliation is

not indiscrimination but «unity in reconciled diversity».

4. Regarding the *concept of church*, the contrast between «state church» (literally: *Volkskirche* or people's church) and «confessing church» is a simplified approximation, as if in the Anabaptist perspective there were no «people» and as if the freedom to confess in the Reformed tradition would eliminate the responsibility of the church to confess!

5. Each trend must deal with both aspects *in their own way:* creative witnessing and free, responsible contact with the public.

6. A relatively open and formally regulated *membership* (in extreme cases only through church taxation) allows the differentiation between visible and invisible church to be maintained, yet brings with it the danger of non-commitment. A relatively strict membership based on voluntary involvement causes obligation, but hides the danger of people being caught in this freedom of choice and it becoming forced.

7. The Anabaptist tradition tends towards a direct statement, which desires *word and faith* in lived out authenticity to appear (danger of external superficiality). For the Reformed tradition, word and faith are objects of an indirect statement, following the conviction that each person should take their position in freedom (danger of internal spiritualization).

8. The Reformed church desires to address people as broadly as possible and therefore goes to great lengths to speak the *language* of these people; however, the danger in this regard is to lose clarity. The Anabaptist church ex-

presses its message with a tradition-oriented language which achieves clarity, but raises the hurdle of understanding for outsiders.

9. The Reformed tradition has emphasized *child baptism* as a sign of the unconditional grace of God, but today, with a diminishing relationship with the people, it is discovering *adult baptism* to be a sign of a binding responsibility to the faith. The Anabaptist tradition has understood adult baptism to be the believer's profession of responsibility; today, however, it has discovered the task of embedding family life in the modern world into the assurance of the love of God. (The consecration of infants might in fact be seen as a quasi-baptism.)

10. In regard to *contact with the public*, the Anabaptist movement makes it their business to express contrast to the world (antitheses to the Sermon on the Mount), thereby encouraging withdrawal from the world (the free church as a «world-free» church?). The Reformed church sees itself closely bound to the world, society, the state (state church), but also falls easily under suspicion of secularization.

11. The Reformed church lives from a tradition of *majority church*, but could increasingly be confronted by the difficulties of a minority church. The Anabaptist church sees itself traditionally as a *minority church*, but could increasingly be confronted with the challenges of a majority church. They should help each other at possible intersections of these developments to better discern their responsibilities.

Inauguration of the Memorial Plaque at the Limmat River, June 26, 2004

Photo Seven: Memorial plaque at the Limmat River in Zurich.

«FROM A FISHING PLATFORM
HERE IN THE MIDDLE OF THE LIMMAT
    FELIX MANZ AND FIVE OTHER ANABAPTISTS WERE
    DROWNED BETWEEN 1527 AND 1532
    DURING THE TIME OF THE REFORMATION.
THE LAST ANABAPTIST TO BE EXECUTED
IN ZURICH WAS HANS LANDIS IN 1614.»

Introduction by Philippe Dätwyler

Here we stand. On this memorable Saturday in the year of our Lord, 2004, we look over the Limmat, which flows calmly, reflecting the evening light.

Here, at this place 477 years earlier, stood many people: councilmen, bystanders and onlookers. It was cold on that day, literally and figuratively. It was January 5, 1527. A Saturday like today. It was the day before Three King's Day. On this day, Felix Manz, the first of seven Anabaptists to be executed in Zurich, was drowned.

In the middle of October 1526, the Zurich authorities had decreed that those who teach and practice adult baptism, and who continue to meet for this purpose will be punished by death.

A few weeks later, in December, Felix Manz was arrested and thrown into the city prison, into the so-called Wellenberg tower. This was a stone tower in the middle of the Limmat.

In prison, Felix Manz remained steadfast in his opinion. He said that he would continue to practice believer's baptism because it is biblical. The authorities probably wanted to make an example of Manz as a dire warning to other Anabaptists.

The church cooperated, too. Two days before the drowning of Felix Manz, Zwingli wrote to Oekolampad, the reformer at Basel: «The Anabaptists, who should already have been sent to the devil, disturb the peace of the pious people. But I believe, the ax will settle it.»

Manz was taken out of the Wellenberg prison and led to the fish market by the Limmat. There his death sentence was read. He was taken to the butcher shop, and then forced into a boat, in which the executioner and a pastor were standing.

Not only did Zwingli seem to know what was going to happen on that Saturday. He had also endorsed it. Heinrich Bullinger describes the martyrdom of Felix Manz, January 5, 1527, in his *Chronicle of the Reformation* this way:

According to Bullinger, it was while he was on this painful course that Felix Manz met his mother and his brother, who encouraged him to remain steadfast and faithful. Then he was brought in the boat to this place. At that time there was a small fishing hut located in the middle of the river.

Felix Manz was placed on the platform of the hut, where his hands were shackled and (while seated) pulled over his knees. Then a stick was inserted under his knees and over his arms so that he was even more securely bound. And as the executioner performed his duty, so the story goes, Manz cried out with loud voice, *Domine in Manus tuas commendo spiritum meum*, «Lord, into your hands I commend my spirit.»

Then using ropes the executioner pulled him off the platform of the fishing hut, down in the cold water of the Limmat.

Robert Neukomm, Member of the City Council

Today, with the unveiling of the memorial plaque for Felix Manz and the other Anabaptists who were drowned at this location in the Limmat River, we would like to set in place a sign of reconciliation. It is a sincere desire of the Zurich City Council to take part in this act (which they do through my representation, let it be noted, as I am a Reformed member of the Council). And the sign of reconciliation between the Council and the Anabaptists of the entire world is in fact a double one for them: a larger sign and a smaller one.

The larger sign of reconciliation refers to the murder of Felix Manz and at least six other Anabaptists. However, it also refers to the persecution and expulsion of countless Anabaptists in Zurich and its surroundings during the Reformation and in the post-Reformation era. The Zurich Council of that time carries the responsibility for this injustice. They pronounced the death sentence, they ordered the persecutions. In the end, the Reformed church delivered to them the necessary visible arguments for it. In any case, one needs no special understanding of history, but only a little political knowledge to recognize that these atrocities resulted not primarily due to religious reasons, but resulted instead from the reasons of the state of that time. On the one hand, in the eyes of the Zurich Council, the Reformed Zurich could not afford an inner division of its own population in the face of the threat of the Catholic cantons, without putting the entire Reformation work – and with it also the state church – in danger. On the other hand, the Anabaptists (almost three hundred years before the French Revolution!) represented revolutionary thinking regarding the relationship between citizens and state and social questions, which the then feudal and corporate authorities could not and would not tolerate.

The smaller sign of reconciliation refers to the refusal of the Zurich City Council to display this plaque here in the year 1952. This decision (seven years after the bitter experience of the Holocaust!) is hardly comprehensible today … The discussions must have been fierce. The decisive question apparently was whether people, whose words and actions were directed against the state at that time (whether Felix Manz, respectively the Anabaptists really did this was not a question), today should receive a memorial plaque or not.

The current Zurich City Council did not discuss whether a memorial plaque for Felix Manz and the other Anabaptists is appropriate or not. It reminds us too much and too painfully of the events, in particular of the 20th century, in which millions of people were killed due to reasons of the state, which have been glossed over with religious arguments in Europe and in other places. It even reminds us of recent or present events such as in Chechnya, Afghanistan, Iraq, Palestine, Sudan or the Balkans, to name only a few, where today war and deadly conflicts are fought and people are executed in the name of reasons of the state and also of religion.

Photo Eight: A sailor in traditional clothing unveils the memorial plaque on the Limmat.

Commemorative plaques are not only responsible for reminding us of events in the past. They are not only responsible for calling us to reconciliation when they remind us of previous atrocities. They should also point us to the path for a better future. In this concrete case, this commemorative plaque should also remind us that reasons of the state and religious conflicts must never be imposed over human rights.

In this sense, the Zurich City Council (as indirect successor of the Zurich Council of that time, but also as the successor of the 1952 City Council) asks the Anabaptists for forgiveness for the atrocities done to them. The Council hopes and expresses its commitment to ensure that this or similar cases of injustice never occur again. The Council is reaching out its hand in reconciliation and would be grateful if you would grasp it.

Ruedi Reich, President of the Council of the Evangelical-Reformed Church of the Canton of Zurich

Dear sisters and brothers,

We commemorate here our brothers in Christ who were cruelly tortured and executed for their faith during the Reformation. The Reformation in Zurich regarded itself as a rediscovery of the liberating Gospel of Jesus Christ. For this, the members of the newly forming Reformed church were also ready to give up their lives.

We are therefore all the more ashamed and pained that the Reformed church should have become a persecutor. In the Zurich of the Reformation, our brothers in the faith of Anabaptist convictions were persecuted, tortured and cruelly executed in a combined action by church and state. We acknowledge this historic sin and, from today's point of view, consider it a betrayal of the Gospel. Before God and before men, we point to this dark side of the Reformation, and we ask God and you, dear brothers and sisters of the Mennonite faith, to forgive us. We are grateful for the fellowship with the Mennonites in the past and today. In the midst of a violent world, we wish to work together for peace, reconciliation and justice. May this reconciliation

93

with each other give us the strength to work together commissioned by Jesus Christ as agents of reconciliation, in small things and in great ones. For this, we ask God's blessing with all our heart.

Thomas Gyger, President of the Swiss Mennonite Conference

Mr. City Councilor, dear members of the Reformed church, our brothers and sisters in Christ,

Though the persecution of the Anabaptists was an outright injustice, we realize that what first motivated the authorities in the 16th century was to maintain public order. In a society where the church and the state were united in a single «Christianity», we understand that when our ancestors rebaptized adults who wished to be converted, they were considered a serious threat.

By inaugurating this memorial plaque in the exact same place where Felix Manz and his friends received the blood baptism, and by reaffirming in a lasting form that your predecessors were wrong in the way they treated these dissidents, you are acting in order to re-establish justice. Your predecessors acted by necessity, you, however, act freely without being forced to.

In the name of my Mennonite brothers and sisters coming from different horizons, I would like to express my gratitude to the authorities of the city of Zurich, as well as to those of the Reformed Church of the Canton of Zurich. For some of us, this plaque represents a way of perpetrating the memory of our past and, we hope, the dialogue; others see in it the strong sign of an important event that tomorrow will be over, but that we will refer to in order to testify of our reconciliation.

Photo Nine: Ruedi Reich (left) and Thomas Gyger at the inauguration of the memorial plaque.

Today, Zurich has become a prosperous and flourishing city where rebaptisms should no longer disturb the public order. However, what would this city be without divine grace and generations of men and women filled with the word of God, and with Judaeo-Christian values? At one time divided, we want today in the midst of our society, to join our voices to yours, dear Reformed friends, in order to repeat together the message of Him who touches and transforms hearts, who is no other than Jesus Christ, our Lord.

From the Old Order Amish Churches of the USA

To the Reformed Church of Zurich:

Heartfelt friendly greetings in Jesus Christ, the Savior's name with best wishes in both time and eternity.

We, the Old Order Churches of the USA have received at hand an invitation by the Reformed Church of Zurich to participate in a conference planned for the weekend of June 26 this year. We acknowledge the motive of such a conference. However, anyone well acquainted with the Old Order Amish will be aware that world travel is not in accordance with our culture. It would take a drastic occurrence to induce delegates of the more conservative Amish to travel to Switzerland. We cannot speak for the more progressive or New Order groups

How do we feel toward the Reformed church? We feel the same about the Reformed church as we do about all other Protestant and Christian churches. We hold a considerable value on any church that teaches its followers to fear God and live in peace with their fellowmen. This earth is a better place to live because of the various Christian churches and their principles.

We believe the descendants of the Reformed churches are not accountable for any actions their forefathers took against the Anabaptists. Far be it from us to request reconciliation. History teaches us that a church is made stronger by persecution. The blood of the martyrs became the seed of the church. We wonder if there would be any Amish, Mennonite or Hutterite churches today if there had not been any persecution. Christ forbids us to hold ill feelings toward the descendants of any oppressors, whether they are Reformed, Catholic, Jew or heathen. We hold this to be the general feeling of the Amish in the USA, consisting of over 1,000 churches, and averaging 25 to 30 families each.

Whenever mention is made of our fatherland, the first to come to mind for most of us, is Switzerland, together with Germany, Holland and France.

Please accept this humble writing in good faith. We hold no ill feelings and plead forbearance for any grievance we may have caused.

God bless you and yours. Fare thee well

John T. Petersheim, Mifflinton, PA
John S. Stoltzfus; Samuel K. Lapp; Jacob N. Peachey;
Abraham S. Renno; Joseph E. Swarey; Dan D. Kurtz

Index of Illustrations

Title page: Execution of Jakob Falk and Heini Reimann 1528, one-and-a-half years after Felix Manz, by drowning in the Limmat River, pushed off the platform of a fisherman's hut. Source: From the Reformation History by Heinrich Bullinger, written and illustrated by Heinrich Thomann. Zurich Central Library, Ms B 316, sheet 336v.

Photos no. 1, 3, 4, 5, 7, 8, 9: refbild, Gion Pfander.

Photo no. 2: Peter Dettwiler.

Photo no. 6: Zurich Central Library, LKS 91 FBQ.

Source Details

Mennonites and Reformed –
A Process of Reconciliation

First published in *Commemorating Witnesses and Martyrs of the Past – a Reformed Perspective*. Edited by Lukas Vischer. John Knox Series no. 17, Geneva 2006. Topic of the booklet: «To what extent can the great witnesses of the past become a common treasure of the divided churches? Though the Reformed were often the victims of persecutions, they have also acted as persecutors.»

In collaboration with Hanspeter Jecker, Professor at the Bienenberg Mennonite Seminary, from a compilation by Sabine Herold, 2003.

Reconciliation? A Mennonite Statement

Abridged and revised edition of an article from *notabene*, 2/2004, published by the Evangelical-Reformed Church of the Canton of Zurich, Church Information Services.

The Anabaptist Inheritance in Ecumenical Dialogue – A Reformed Perspective
Abridged and revised edition of a lecture held on September 10, 2005 in Tavannes, at the meeting of the elders and ministers of the Swiss Mennonite Conference.

The Confession and its Significance
Abridged and revised edition of an article written for the occasion of the study day in Augsburg on November 12, 2005 with the title: *«Waging Lawful War or Opposing It»* – The ecumenical Decade to Overcoming Violence and Article 16 of the Augsburg Confession, Work Group 4: Two types of dealing with Reformed confessions, comparison of the Lutheran with the Reformed approaches to the confessions.

New Horizons
Abridged articles from: *Mennonite Historical Bulletin,* October 2004, no. 4. The article by J. Ebersole from February 2007 is a personal contribution.

«They too are Reformed»
Abridged article from the *Reformierte Presse* (*Reformed Press*) 27/2004.

Details about the Authors

Michael Baumann: Minister of the Evangelical-Reformed Church of the Canton of Zurich and Reformation historian.

Pierre Bühler: Professor of Systematic Theology at the University of Zurich.

Philippe Dätwyler: Cultural representative of the Evangelical-Reformed Church of the Canton of Zurich and initiator of the conference of June 26, 2004, «The Reformation and the Anabaptists. Steps to Reconciliation.»

Peter Dettwiler: Ecumenical representative of the Evangelical-Reformed Church of the Canton of Zurich. Member of the planning committee for the conference of June 26, 2004.

Jon M. Ebersole: Mediator, developmental coach, Affoltern am Albis, Switzerland.

Ernest Geiser: President of the Council of Elders of the Swiss Mennonite Conference.

Thomas Gyger: President of the Swiss Mennonite Conference 2002–2004. Member of the planning committee for the conference of June 26, 2004.

Hanspeter Jecker: Professor at the Bienenberg Theological Seminary in Switzerland and Co-President of the Swiss Association for Anabaptist History. Member of the planning committee for the conference of June 26, 2004.

Stephan Landis: Editor at the *Reformierte Presse (Reformed Press)*, linguist and theologian.

Larry Miller: Dr., General Secretary of the Mennonite World Conference.

Robert Neukomm: Member of the Zurich City Council since 1990. Chairman of the Health and Environment Department.

Dan Nighswander: General Secretary of Mennonite Church Canada.

Ruedi Reich: Rev. Dr. h.c., President of the Council of the Evangelical-Reformed Church of the Canton Zurich since 1993.

John D. Rempel: Assistant Professor of Historical Theology at Associated Mennonite Biblical Seminary since 2003.

John E. Sharp: Director of Goshen Archives, Historical Committee, Mennonite Church, USA. Member of the planning committee for the conference of June 26, 2004.

Franklin Yoder: Academic advisor at the University of Iowa and Chair of the Mennonite Church USA Historical Committee.